# Covert Technological Murder

## Pain Ray Beam

RENEE PITTMAN

Mother's Love Publishing and Enterprises

**ISBN 13:** 978-1-7374060-2-0

# <u>DEDICATION</u>

This book is dedicated to the global effort of exposure, and continued hope for help for victims non-consensually used, at this very moment, in one of the most unimaginable and heinous Crime of the Century, in a program with tendrils, dating back many years.

Give me liberty or give me death! Since this operation cannot come into the open without revealing themselves 100%.


What will they choose?

iv

# TABLE OF CONTENTS

# ACKNOWLEDGMENT

During a Coast to Coast interview, August 27, 2013, titled Electronic Harassment, 300,000 was the number given regarding those suffering electromagnetic technology attacks within America. However, many suspect the number is far greater and continues to grow.

My voice and experiences alone are just not enough when making these types of claims. Indeed, one person making such claims, historically, and today, has gotten them one thing, and one thing only, an involuntary stay in the psyche ward and indefinitely if those targeting the individual has anything to do with it.

It is my continued belief that by adding my voice to thousands of others, and continuing to compile just a tiny portion of the extensive research material available, for substantiation, along with the personal experiences of Targeted Individuals, that through our unified effort we will effect change to these horrendous secret crimes of physical torture and psychological abuse and covert manipulation.

I, acknowledge this information is not news to those that are targeted. My target is those, who do not have a clue why suddenly their health begins to deteriorate, forced to do this type of research necessary to gain an understanding of how just to survive.

# INTRODUCTION

I n June of 2013, I continued to search for solutions to the torture and abuse I and many are experiencing around the clock. I thought a book detailing victim experiences, other than my own, might prove effective in helping the cause. When looking for solutions, I reasoned, the effort must be to bring what is happening today to mainstream America and hope to rally the support of the general public regarding this specific type of covert abuse being inflicted in various forms on the human body and through various methods.

I did get a few responses from targeted individuals all over the country, however, many, after showing initial interest in the project later declined. One individual reported that soon after considering it those monitoring him immediately began an effort to persuade him to not get involved. He reported that the microwave Directed Energy Weapon attacks escalated in his life and he now felt it too costly, both mentally and physically, to participate. In other words, a clear message had been sent from the operation center that in doing so, it would be detrimental to his mental and physical health to an advanced extreme.

I, of all people, completely understood his position and subsequent decline and not wanting to be involvement as a result. I had suffered, and continue to suffer, both mental and physical attacks and abuse by the military and law enforcement group assigned to me on a daily basis.

One person, whose story I accidentally stumbled upon a few years back during an internet search, was that of Jeremiah Ivie. Jeremiah is a little-known activist today; was making waves, by working tirelessly to expose the misuse of electromagnetic technology of which he has firsthand experience at a horrific level.

When I read his personal account of electromagnetic mind control and electromagnetic weapon attacks and successful subliminal manipulation, before he woke up, I was greatly moved. In fact, it brought tears to my eyes to hear of such cruelty. After hearing what happened to him and his parents, I declared, in my own suffering and fight, that I would do everything within my limited power to expose what today is a program that has morphed into a legalized, unrestrained, government approved, technology testing amped on steroids.

The fact that it is little known to the general public and 100% legally approved by exceptions for the military for research activity and law enforcement for biological crowd control makes it secretly dangerous. Because it is not being broadcast, human suffering by these two groups is thriving as a fully mobilized global effort.

A few months after my request on Facebook for victim stories, Jeremiah Ivie and I connected in a joint effort to publicize the beginning of the mind control attempt in his life, his suffering, plight, and ultimate redemption. I am grateful for his bravery and brutal honesty in detailing his specific situation.

The theory behind mind control technology is that the bioelectric brain emits electromagnetic energy and by using an electroencephalogram (EEG) brainwaves can be detected, translated into a vocabulary, and used for monitoring and analysis. Computers can correlate behavior and speech to the brainwave signals and the mind and thoughts of the victim can be remotely deciphered. Mind reading is pivotal for those at the helm of these advancements through the vital awareness of knowing what is effective with victims and the focused hope to push victims over the edge. For example, with a woman, while they learn after beamed focused to the breast is creating fear or rightful concern, this area will become an area of primary focus.

This theory also works in reverse. In stimulating or controlling human behavior, the brain communicates via electromagnetic signals. Decades of scientific research has proven that manipulation of certain electromagnetic frequencies creates and correspond with specific mood states, changes and behavior. The brain cannot differentiate a foreign signal from its own.

By targeting the subconscious mind with messages as hypnotists does, for example, the technology can remotely target the subconscious mind and it becomes a very potent mind control weapon.

"The Mind has no Firewall. - Therefore, is susceptible to all form of non-detectable intrusions." If your thoughts were hacked you wouldn't even know they weren't your own. --- Timothy L Thomas (The U.S. Army War College Quarterly)

This is a simple explanation of complex electromagnetic technology. However, in present day, with then President Bush proclaiming the 1990s the Decade of the Brain, it is well within the realm of reality. One of the best books on this topic is Dr. Becker's The Body Electric: Electromagnetism and The Foundation of Life, published in 1985.

Many victims are grateful for Jeremiah courageously detailing his story. He and his parents suffered a great deal. He, as does many, realize that in order to draw attention to what is really happening in these vicious scientific programs, to include the capability and characteristics of powerful electromagnetic influencing technology, victims must be strong and brave enough to fully exposed, no matter how distasteful, or embarrassing, the levels of humiliation, and depravity that those at the helm of the technology will go to.

These programs have thrived for decades due to continued disbelief, discrediting, unheard of personal humiliation silencing, threats, covert barbaric torture, and most of all through the creation of emotional fear, anger, anxiety, hatred, covertly beamed extreme stress in many forms through manipulation of extremely low frequencies as a method for control and forcing victims to comply.

Personally, after writing "Remote Brain Targeting" Book I, used as the blueprint by detailing, research, testing and development historic programs leading up to full implementation of this technology, then "You Are Not My Big Brother" detailing my personal experiences, I hoped that the effort around me would dim somewhat due to exposure. To my chagrin, this would not be the case. Because those in these programs are operating under Color of Law, and are protected by laws approving technology testing intentionally enacted after 9/11, two things became obvious to me,

(1) The group targeting me, working around the clock, now entering its eighth year in 2014, believed that eventually they would torture me into submission as well by getting me to react negatively.

(2) And that 24/7/365 slow kill death by constant irradiation of a target's body, that the goal of silencing would be inevitable or at the very least shorten my lifespan.

Admittedly, a couple of times, due to the relentless attempts to torture me into submission, program me and break my will, the thought had materialized in my head that I could not take the horrendous pain and debilitating torture by microwave directed energy weapons, or the intense psychological accompanied verbal abuse and that I should just rest in peace by suicide. However, the realization of the definite technological capability to influence a target by implanting thoughts directly into the human brain cautioned me bringing me back to reality.

I would also have to come to terms with a fact of which many targets, past and present and likely future will agree or learn, once you are placed into this type of highly technical program, it usually is for the rest of your life and the same people are around you day and night for years through their employment and when they retired someone else takes over.

The capabilities of numerous electromagnetic patented devices, software, and state-of-the-art computer systems, continues to be beyond belief or comprehension for the average American. This is in spite of numerous official patents for these technologies, backed by documented official laws approving its use.

Nudging a person to end their own life by suicide through the technological powerful electromagnetic influencing affect is just as sure as murdering someone as pulling the trigger although done using the highly advanced global weapon system, drones, satellite biometric EEG tracking of human targets, and torture through antenna topped cellular towers when driving, a fixed with microwave directed energy weapons along with the Ground Wave Energy Network is real. When traveling from state-to-state or country to country advanced technologies are being deployed by a constellation of satellites and through a large phased array of terrestrial antennas.

Satellites and drones are also being used for infrared imaging and visual imaging of this integrated global surveillance system.

There are reports, stating that over 20,000 satellites currently target and silence countless people worldwide (est. 500,000 plus) as a result of bad laws. The victims are not openly confronted. This would remove any feigned excuses and leave the perpetrators open to all manner of accusation. Instead the methods used are covert; employing high tech' systems to remotely torment and deceive victims without leaving evidence.

Often targets are tricked into believing they are having psychic, medical, psychiatric, religious, or even alien experiences (which they are not) says Paul Baird, an Australian activist. This leaves them discredited as they vainly seek help from ignorant or complicit authorities (police, military personnel, doctors, media, etc.). This leaves victims neutralized and possibly even silenced on the issue they originally raised.

The question still remains, what would make people, law enforcement and the military, at the helm of this technology, or even the average American citizen trained by Intel agencies during Community Stalking as vigilantes using portable versions, become so ruthless, and eagerly partake in such vicious life-threatening cruelty, without guilt, perpetrating crimes against another human being, while not wanting it known, or you to see their faces? Have they lost and or now devoid of how wrong it is? One, factor is the great difficulty in proving what is happening to targets which seems to be a source of great amusement not to mention security for some of the more sadistic individuals working in these programs for hire. Some, I believe, also enjoy the power of influencing and controlling another's life or essentially playing God to a lesser degree driven by a psychopathic mentality.

There are three specific technologies in use today primarily from state-of-the-art operation centers with, powered by the availability of numerous other patents known as "Black Bag" technologies. That is first, artificial/synthetic telepathy, also known as the hearing voices effect, voice to skull, or neural decoding, and Electroencephalogram (EEG), incorporating mind reading technology, as stated vital and necessary to harass the target. The technology is so advanced that EEG Cloning, by capturing a specific negative emotion can be stored into a highly advanced supercomputer system then believe it or not, beamed back to the victim creating negative emotions materialized out of nowhere and effortlessly.

The numbers continue to grow with people, for example in cities such as Palm Springs, California, experiencing the "Synthetic Telepathy" effect reported on a KMIR 6 news report. To the advantage of this gay community obviously marked for experimentation, their recognizing that they were being targeted by technology as a group resulted in their knowing they were not crazy it saved their lives. This report is a good example of the ability to manipulate specific groups and populations by individuals working from a centralized location.

Also, in December of 2012, TruTV, Conspiracy Theory, with Jesse Ventura, and episode preserved on Daily Motions, "Brain Invader" premiered an episode spotlighting complaints within America focused on electronic harassment also through synthetic beamed voices inside their heads again, originating from state-of-the-art operation centers, drones, along with deadly microwave torture inside their homes and out. The show was entitled "Brain Invaders."

The Palm Springs, California investigative news report, through KMIR6.com is titled – "Electronic Harassment: Voices in My Mind" by Angela Monroe, Nov. 12, 2012 if you should desire to look it up for yourself.

The article begins by saying "Hundreds of people in the valley say they are hearing voices in their heads, and those voices are being transmitted by microwave or other methods..."

The question is, just how long did those having full knowledge of the development and use of various electromagnetic technologies today, that resonate bio-electrically resulting in mind invasions, expect to keep the general public in the dark. Obviously, these programs believed that the general public would not begin to come to the same conclusion in realization that something else is afoot?

As with, myself and others, most people know themselves and as a result can easily distinguish when something is thought completely out of character and it is just not right and deviant from their typical feelings which have been a part of their lives, and thought process throughout their lives. Through our specific personality characteristics, likes and dislikes, essentially in effect since birth, any deviant thought most recognize can be a dead giveaway, forgive the pun, that something is amidst, especially when combined with the myriad of documented, and detailed information, readily available today for the inquiring mine seeking substantiation.

As I read through the Palm Springs, California article, as a native of California, I was struck by a realistic statement made by a person identified as Dr. Drucker.

He stated, "That testing appears to be happening to people that are marginalized, deemed valueless, are easy targets with testing factually occurring in an entire community."

Remember this is mass control technology, intentionally and specifically designed for this sole purpose and designed with characteristics for global control ultimately as its endeavor. This is known to those familiar with and understand its history.

The key to the continued success of these programs is discrediting the targets as nutcases. I myself, continue to personally question why, psychiatry can easily ignore literally hundreds of official patents, patented at the United States Patent and Trademark Office, and definite laws approving use of this technology so easily. How, also, can they deny or write off the reports of highly educated individuals and even historical archived documentation declassified?

Many are reporting similar experiences across the board today although at different and varying levels which appears to be structured by the target's specific involvement and why they are placed in this program. These highly educated people can't be nor are they so stupid. Or perhaps self-serving may be a better definition or lack of awareness key.

In reality, historically, the Association of Psychiatry, as I documented in the first book in this series, continues to play, a pivotal role in remote neural monitoring also known as "Remote Brain Targeting" programs with studies justified in the name of science. Traditionally, many in this field, although not all, have been a part of the problem and not the solution in the arena of behavior studies for decades. Donald Ewen Cameron spearheaded early studies, as president of the American Association of Psychiatry in both the USA and Canada for MKULTRA mind control studies

Stating that this program is "a waking nightmare" by one of the victims in the article is an understatement. It is a technological monster using highly advanced mega computer systems, of which one author defines as having such acronyms as Thought Amplifier and Mind

Interface or T.A.M.I or Global Orbit Directed Energy Weapon System or G.O.D.S.

M.I.N.D, believed to be the name of the top-secret project of electromagnetic mind control, reported by insiders, as the Magnetic Integrated Neuron Duplicator. It appears this is a system of artificial intelligence with many aspects of not only efficient EEG cloning. SATAN appears to be appropriately named. SATAN is said to be the name of the kill mode weaponized software of this high-tech system or Silent Assassination through Amplified Neurons. And, SATAN is said to be housed in a location called HELL, again name appropriate and possibly intentionally.

By using brain interfaced super computer-enhanced EEGs, scientists have identified, and have isolated the brain's low-amplitude "emotion signature clusters" as stated previously. They have synthesized them and stored them into a mega computer / Brain Computer Interface or BCI system.

These clusters are then placed onto an extremely low frequency carrier system, for example the Silent Sound Spread Spectrum, which is capable of carrying extremely low frequencies which are EEG Cloned for global manipulation if necessary through radio waves. For example, the emotions of millions can be captured and beamed back to millions. Studies show through, for example, the television pulsing electromagnetic frequencies.

# Nervous system manipulation by electromagnetic fields from monitors

**Patent number: 6506148**

**Abstract:** Physiological effects have been observed in a human subject in response to stimulation of the skin with weak electromagnetic fields that are pulsed with certain frequencies near ½ Hz or 2.4 Hz, such as to excite a sensory resonance. Many computer monitors and TV tubes, when displaying pulsed images, emit pulsed electromagnetic fields of sufficient amplitudes to cause such excitation. It is therefore possible to manipulate the nervous system of a subject by pulsing images displayed on a nearby computer monitor or TV set. For the latter, the image pulsing may be imbedded in the program material, or it may be overlaid by modulating a video stream, either as an RF signal or as a video signal. The image displayed on a computer monitor may be pulsed effectively by a simple computer program. For certain monitors, pulsed electromagnetic fields capable of exciting sensory resonances in nearby subjects may be generated even as the displayed images are pulsed with subliminal intensity.

**Type:** Grant

**Filed:** June 1, 2001

**Date of Patent:** January 14, 2003

**Inventor:** Hendricus G. Loos

Many Targeted Individuals who have survived the strategic discrediting phase has experienced emotional cloning of fear repeatedly. When the technology is used this way, the cloned emotion can silently trigger the occurrence of the same type of emotion in a Target or targets, as shown by the patent cast over large populations, individuals or groups and typically negative emotions such as creating riots.

Let me state for the record, and from personal experience, those involved with the use of this technology are not interested in sending happy feelings of joy to individuals unless it is beneficial to their cause or the program statistics overall.

As I have previously documented, in one of the other two books, The Silent Sound Spread Spectrum or SSSS sometimes called "S-quad" or "Squad" is a mind-altering mechanism based on a patented subliminal carrier technology first on the scene during the Eisenhower Administration of the late 50s and early 60s. An example of the Silent Sounds Subliminal System capability might utilize voice commands, e.g., as an adjunct to a security system for example. For example, when entering Walmart, or beneath the musical broadcast that you hear in stores and shopping malls may be a hidden message which exhorts against shoplifting subliminally by bypassing the outer ear as a suggestion beamed directly into the human brain. And while voice commands alone are powerful, when the subliminal presentation system carries cloned emotional signatures, for an individual, population, or group targeted in this manner, the results could be overwhelmingly heinous to say the least not to mention ungodly.

If the names of these top-secret mind invasive, mentally, physically and emotionally weapon system are accurate the very names paint a perfect picture of purpose, capability, and more importantly, the intent.

The edge of those working these operations, nationwide, depending on the level a target has advanced to, is the threat of death from coercive energy weapon physical torture covertly beamed simultaneously with beamed fear to psychologically control the victim's actions.

I will say this again, and again, "Fear has never conquered anything!"

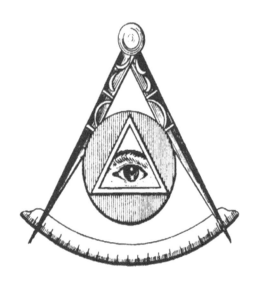

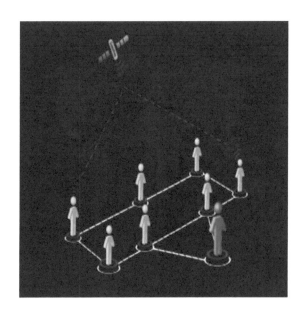

# CHAPTER ONE
# Ancient History and Electromagnetic Energy

L ightening is the most dramatic form of energy to be found in nature. Scientist has succeeded in creating limited types of artificial lightening, the forerunner for Directed Energy Weapons. These weapons operate within the Radio Frequency segment of the Electromagnetic Spectrum and can be deadly.

The ancient Egyptians had many advanced scientific technologies. Much of what they did has been found in picture form as hieroglyphics and three-dimensional models throughout Egypt. Actual themes reflecting scientific knowledge and achievement can be found through the world in scenery about ancient civilizations. Their teachings seemed to center on electromagnetic energies.

Scenes depict scientists of that timeline able to work in fields of alchemy, biology, chemistry, dentistry, anesthesiology, air flight, and electromagnetic energies, as imagery on the walls of the Great Pyramid. This is common among other sacred sites with imagery defining links to the sacred geometry that forms our universe. However, much of the interpretation today is left to those in our timeline to decipher, although a common practice for the neophyte of Mystery School, esoteric knowledge of secret societies.

The "Energy Source" The Wands of Horus & the Structures of Deep Meditation were a foundation for spiritual practices in Ancient Egypt.

For long millennia, the great pyramids preserved the mystery of a "secret room" containing, according to legend, either secrets of a special kind of knowledge that would give the finder power over the world.

Men have been searching for that knowledge for many centuries and it appears today believe they have honed the Earth's energy source or what Nikola Tesla called "Radiant Energy" by advanced technological use. The fact is there is nothing new under the Sun.

The scholar has looked for it within the twin-humped rock on which the body of the pyramid rests. They looked for it beneath the pyramid. But the room is not where they were looking but in the upper part of the pyramid, at a point defined by the ratio 0.118:0.882. That chamber contains the "Energy Source" of which the Ancient Egyptians inherited from the people of Atlantis who had come to northern Africa long before the heyday of Egyptian civilization.

The founders of Atlantis were said to be half god and half human. They were said to have created a utopian civilization and became a great naval power. Their home was made up of concentric islands separated by wide moats and linked by a canal that penetrated to the center. The lush islands contained gold, silver, and other precious metals and supported an abundance of rare, exotic wildlife. There was a great capital city on the central island.

The energy source takes the form of a cylinder within which is a special crystal with a lattice structure close in parameters to that of quartz crystals. Almost all the most astonishing phenomena observed in and around the pyramid are connected with the presence of this very device. The sense of creating and using the "Energy Source" lies in its capacity to affect the structure of time and space in the vicinity of its location. The shape of the pyramid serves to intensify this effect and disperses the incoming energy in the area of the pyramid.

Besides that, this "Energy Source" was known to affect, not only human psychological but also physical structure.

Pick up any book about Ancient Egyptian culture and take a close look at the statues of the pharaohs: you will see that they are all clasping cylinder-like objects in their hands.

The "Energy Source" that was constructed in the proportions of the Golden Section entered into resonant interaction with the cylinders held in the hands because they too were created in the proportions of the Golden Section. In other words, there was an electromagnetic connection simply by holding the object to draw the Energy Source.

Apart from that, however, both these devices, the Energy Source and Golden Section, were constructed, one might say, in a single image and likeness as a kind of miniature model of certain energy processes that arise cyclically in the biosphere and the space around a human being. That, in turn, determines yet another level of interaction between them.

Those cylinders, with which the pharaohs never parted throughout their lives, were harmonizers of the two basic flows of energy which the Ancient Egyptians called BA and KA, corresponding to Yin and Yang in the Oriental tradition.

For the Ancient Egyptians BA and KA were the two component elements of the human entity, the two sources of vital energy. Later, much of this knowledge was then transferred to Ancient Greece.

Man's first awareness of electromagnetic phenomena probably started with the very dawn of civilization. About 600 BC Thales of Miletus, a Greek philosopher, noted that a piece of amber could be made to attract small particles by rubbing it with cloth. Aristotle, in 400 BC, maintained that a force could not be communicated between bodies other than by some tangible means as pressure or impact. Lucretius of Magnesia (98-55 BC) noted the power of lodestone to attract iron.

Thales of Meletus

Aristotle

Lucretius of Magnesia

More recently, William Gilbert (1544-1603), physician to Queen Elizabeth I, expressed the opinion that electrical phenomena are due to something material which is liberated from bodies when electrified by friction, without any change in form or weight.

Rene Descartes (1596-1650) believed that magnetism consisted of vortexes in an omnipresent aether. The idea was later expressed by Leonhard Euler 1707-1783) and James Clark Maxwell in 1861.

Rene Descartes

Leonhard Euler

James Clark Maxwell

James Clark Maxwell (1831-1879) translated Faraday's experiments in electromagnetism into mathematical notations. Maxwell expressed all the fundamental laws of light, electricity and magnetism in "Maxwell Field Equations." These equations, along with Newton's Laws, the Quantum Theory and the Theory of Relativity, are considered the mathematical foundation of the physical universe.

Karl Friedrick Gauss (1777-1855), German mathematician, made one of the first attempts to deduce the fundamental law of electromagnetic action in terms of an electric field propagated at finite velocity.

The first recorded statement on the subject of electro-magnetism was made by Michael Faraday in 1846, suggesting the propagation of magnetic disturbances by means of transverse vibrations. Faraday's greatest discovery was that of electromagnetic induction.

Through a series of brilliant experiments, Heinrich Hertz (1857-1894) established beyond doubt the electromagnetic nature of light and thereby confirmed Maxwell's Theory.

Guglielmo Marconi (1874-1937) first recognized the possibility of using electromagnetic waves as a means of wireless communication. He built parabolic antennas and moved to higher and higher frequencies eventually reaching 550 MHz

.

Credit for the first waveguide experiments probably belongs to George C. Southworth. In 1920, he measured the wavelength of a high frequency signal on a lecher wire frame in air, and then in a trough of water. After observing evidence of other wavelength components superimposed on those expected in water, Dr. Southworth decided that they were related to the dimensions of the trough. While working for AT&T in 1933, he was able to transmit and receive telegraph signals using 20 feet of 4 and 5-inch diameter pipes.

The beginnings of radar were influenced by Albert H. Taylor and Leo C. Young in 1922 when they noticed an unexpected swell in what had been a steady tone of communication, which then faded coinciding with an object crossing the line of sight between the transmitter and receiver. This phenomenon was related to the need for detection of enemy ships.

Albert H. Taylor

Leo C. Young

Little development of radar occurred until 1934, when the United States Naval Research Laboratory, the Germans, and the British began work on it. The klystron was invented at Stanford University in 1937 by Russell Varian along with Sigurd Varian and W. W. Hansen, with funding by Sperry Gyroscope Company looking for solutions to an instrument landing problem.

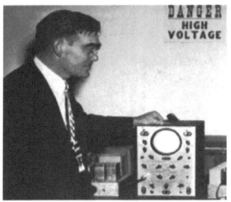

During World War II, Radar became the major application of microwave technology. By 1940, the British had installed a chain of radar installations along the coastline to warn against air attack.

Just prior to World War II, Harry Boot and John Randal invented the 10-cm pulsed-cavity magnetron in England using Hertz's original experiments with loops and gaps as a basis for arranging a number of cylindrical resonators in a circle.

In mid-1940, British personnel led by Sir Henry Tizard brought the device to the U.S. and Canada, initiating the success of Microwave Radar during World War II.

Work was then begun on development of U.S. radar systems, primarily by MIT Radiation Laboratory, but also at other defense industry companies. Many of the subcontracting decisions made then led to the companies' areas of specialization in today's microwave industry.

After World War II, funding for further development in the microwave field was reduced drastically, and research and development efforts over the next 40 years were tied to fluctuations in the U.S. defense budget, with the search for commercial applications occurring generally during low periods in the government demand. Applications developed included communications, commercial radar, industrial heating, and industrial measurements.

## Courtesy National Electronics Museum

Perhaps one of the greatest scientists, not mentioned, who began to connect the dots was Nikola Tesla who patented over 700 inventions related to what he called "Radiant Energy," for example, Tesla coils,

became the foundation for HAARP, and other devices using electromagnetic energy for later for weaponry.

Today electromagnetic energy is the foundation for some of the most advanced weapons on the planet.

# CHAPTER TWO
# Jeremiah's Attempted "False Flag" Programming

J eremiah Ivie appears to be one of the very few who actually got away unscathed, to some degree, before total, efficient collateral damage completely took his life or the lives of his parents by those seeking to use him in what he believes was a False Flag effort.

False flag (or black flag) describes covert military or paramilitary operations designed to deceive society in such a way that the operations appear as though they are being carried out by other entities, groups or nations, other than those who actually planned and executing them. Operations carried out during peace-time by civilian organizations, as well as covert government agencies, may by extension be called false flag operations if they seek to hide the real organization behind an operation. False Flag operations are designed to shake group consciousness in some manner and change the perception of the masses in some way usually for a specific agenda, in most cases, through again, the use of manipulated fear. Some believe such gun control effort to disarm Americans.

Many people in the Targeted Individual Community continue to raise an eyebrow about mass shootings, such as in Aurora, Colorado, James Holmes, and Aaron Alexis, the Washington Navy Yard shooting. In Colorado, the individual responsible had an obvious dumbfounded look on his face while sitting in court and appeared to be in total disbelief himself, that he actually did the things being reported that he had while sitting there in shackles.

There was a Newport, Rhode Island, police report summarizing an early morning complaint in August of 2013 by Washington Navy Yard shooter Aaron Alexis.

Alexis complained that an individual he had an altercation with in an airport had "sent 3 people to follow him and keep him awake by talking to him using 'some sort of microwave device.'" The news report stated.

Was this a first red flag or some would argue, false flag, leading to an alarming portrait of a defense contractor suffering from mental illness? Or fact?

What caused Alexis to voice this complaint on August 7, 2013, 42 days prior to embarking on a shooting rampage at the Navy Yard, leaving 13 workers dead, the location he believed as culprits?

Law enforcement officials close to the investigation have reported to the press that the stock of Alexis' shotgun had been carved with "Better off this way" and "My ELF weapon."

The, Military Industrial Complex, and contractors, many others familiar with this technology know that "ELF" was undoubtedly a reference to "extremely low frequency" and is a term applied to microwave technology and this technology is portable, handheld, land, sea and spaced based. And victims, report, being tracking and monitored by operatives also using portable technology originating from the Military Industrial complex.

As documented from my personal experiences, research and documenting the history of this technology and laws approving its use, microwave mind-control technology was developed over fifty years but specifically during the height of the Cold War.

Among the desired effects of microwave weapons are sleep deprivation, a symptom that reports reveal Alexis received treatment for prior to the shootings.

Alexis's reference to "microwave machines" is more than an utterance; the deceased man was familiar with microwave systems beyond the common kitchen appliance and I can personally attest, to not only the capability to be electronically harassed verbally, as can many of sound mind targeted, but also to the slow kill effect of this technology as a coercive weapon.

Jeremiah Ivies' specific horrific testimony of manipulative abuse is so heinous, that it is hard to believe that individuals are sitting in an operation center, watching in real-time with access to the highly advanced versions of this technology, and with some using it for evil and without remorse. In common with many victims, these efforts relentlessly attempted to manipulate Jeremiah, using every aspect of their high-tech techniques until he sought relief believing that if he did what was requested, his covert torment would cease.

Jeremiah can thank a power greater than himself, and the omnipotent Spirit of goodness at his core which pulled him through and allowed him to turn the table not harm those he loves.

Make no mistake about it, this powerful presence within human being is ultimately untouchable.

With that said here is his personal account in his own words:

## Targeting Testimony of Jeremiah Ivie

I was targeted when I came to San Diego in 1999. I have been kept a prisoner here and unable to leave or prosper do to intense no touch remote torture that is ongoing.

I noticed changes in my mind and body first. Intense sexual desire, mentally and physically. I seemed to develop an uncontrollable urge to masturbate. I noticed that my feelings and emotions could not be controlled when around people, even people that I was normally comfortable around like family and friends. For example, when close to my mother or father I would feel a sexual attraction between us or mental imagery of attraction, this was the same between male friends, which had never happened before. I found it strange because for 29 years I have always been attracted to females. This was disturbing.

But more disturbing was the visualizations of negative mental imagery would appear in my mind and triggered by what I looked at in my environment. My thoughts increasingly became negative and family and friends started to notice and treat me different. I could not figure it out. I became more secluded and paranoid because of my changing feelings and fantasies. I became emotionally sensitized. I could not focus or use my time wisely. It became difficult to work or think productively. I could not focus on my school or work because of these distractions. People in my life who were influential and in positions to help me decided against it because of my instability. It drove a wedge between me and my family. We began to develop a sense of resentment at each other. I developed a sense of dependency toward my mother and father. We became angry at each other and I developed a sense of desperation.

At this time, I noticed that certain parts of my body were constricting and in pain. For example, my left arm and shoulder became week and out of place despite how often I worked out. My neck began to hurt and look skinny and unhealthy in the mirror. My throat and lungs became irritated and stressed as if my glands were sick. My hips started to hurt and protrude from my body. My body odor changed and smelled different. My spine tightened and all my bones began to crack. I started getting uncontrollable urges to crack all my bones, especially my spine and neck. I started getting rashes and hard little bumps were coming out of my skin. I felt afflicted.

My parents threw me out and I became homeless. In my environment people would befriend me and then become hostile and say things that only I would know. They would always pop up out of the blue and try to influence me into negative behavior. They would say and do things to me as if they were trying to program me with street theatre. The color red began to stand out every place I went. I got the feeling that

I was being led into a psychological nightmare. I began to hallucinate and stare at objects for long periods of time. My personality began to change. Then for the first time in my life at age 30 I started hearing voices that were not my own. At first, they were nice to me and tried to gain my loyalty by identifying themselves as the United States military. They said to me that my parents were satanic terrorists that were committing internet crimes like child pornography and secretly filming people and making money off of it online. At the time, I had no idea how my parent made their money so I thought it might be a possibility. They said they were a covert operation that needed my help in killing my parents for duty to country and played on my patriotism because of the war on terror. When I refused and said that I did not believe them they became abusive verbally in my head. It seemed I was communicating with a group of military scientists.

They began to humiliate me after every thought. They began injecting me with dreams of violence and drug use. The mental communication was 24/7 from the moment I woke up to the time I went to bed and every night. I was sleeping less and less. When I would close my eyes, I would see in my mind the outline of men masturbating and laughing at me like they were raping me virtually in my third eye. I was so paranoid wherever I went.

I noticed the patterns of traffic, the way people walked and talked in relation to what I was experiencing. I was being followed by white trucks, vans and what seemed to be brand new government cars with tinted windows wherever I would go.

Police were also stalking me all the time. They had me driving to different locations of town getting out and marching around San Diego like a soldier that they were training for some mission. They were injecting different personalities into me. I would laugh, cry, become angry or aggressive, thoughtful, religious, in an instant, and they let it be known that they were in charge. I was experiencing extreme fatigue along with sharp pains and pressure to my head.

After 9 months of this type of remote torture and gang stalking, they convinced me to kill my parents just on the promise of relief and making it stop. I went into my parent's room with a knife and watched them sleep. I broke down crying, woke my parent up and finally told them what I was experiencing. They called 911 and police and ambulance came and took me to the mental ward. This happened 3 times and on the 4th time I stabbed my dad in the chest several times, threw him down the stairs and beat him. I ran to the police station thinking it was over. I turned myself in and police interrogated me.

I told the Chula Vista police during my statement they that I was hearing military voices that ordered me to kill my parents. The Police became angry at me and aggressive. I got scared and asked for a lawyer. I could not control my speech any longer. I was misdiagnosed and incarcerated.

After 3 days inside jail, the voices stopped but only the body pains remained. When I finally integrated back into society, it all started over again and I noticed the same things starting to happen again. This time I felt extreme pain in all of my limbs that mimicked nerve damage. I became bed ridden and lost my job and car. My parents took me in and let me stay in my dad's office. I would only get out of bed to work or look for work. I was shaking so bad that the whole house was vibrating. All my limbs were jerking and I was getting zapped. In 2007, I went to the hospital to get surgery on my neck or I would have died.

After surgery, the voices came back except this time I was familiar with the attack and started doing research and networking with other targets. After doing research I was able to recognize their tactics and adjust to them. I can identify perps and for more detailed description of their mental torture program I can provide upon request.

Sincerely,

Jeremiah Ivie

What was attempted with Jeremiah has a foundation in a program called Project Monarch which began in Nazi German concentration camps originally led by the infamous Dr. Joseph Mengele also known as the Angel of Death because of his preference for horrific torture. Project Monarch is named after the Monarch butterfly symbolizing transformation. It is a method of mind control which is said to be used today by numerous organizations for covert purposes for example to train assassins. Many believe that many transformed individuals are even today being used for various purposes after being subjected to this programming, which results in the development of Alters or multiple personalities. Any of the Alter personalities can then be triggered by their handlers for example through a computer. Another name for this programming is called Slave or Delta Programming.

Project Monarch has connections to project MK-ULTRA studies also, which was a definite and historically documented mind-control program, as stated previously, developed by the CIA, and tested on the military and civilians during the 50, 60, and 70s until the Church Committee Hearings sent the operation underground.

The traumatic, inhumane methods are documented as being astonishingly sadistic and the expected results are horrifying.

After the mind separates, the creation of a mind-controlled slave is achieved which can be triggered at any time to perform any action required by the handler. By some accounts, over 2 million Americans have gone through the horrors of this program. To achieve Monarch programming, as a mind-control technique, an individual, is subjected to the trauma-based transformation in early childhood and is horrendously tortured in many manners, which comprises elements of Satanic Ritual Abuse resulting in synthetic Multiple Personality Disorder when the mind separates for example, by, in the case of children, watching a loved one brutally, and viciously murdered before their very own eyes. The trauma utilizes a combination of psychology, neuroscience, and occult rituals to create within the slaves an alter persona that can be triggered and programmed by the handlers, sleep deprivation, drugs, etc., are also key tools of programming.

Today Monarch slaves are used by several organizations connected with the world elite, and it is believed today in fields ranging from the military, as sex slavery, and throughout the entertainment industry. Many have seen images of their favorite entertainers covering one eye, or displaying the three sixes sign, which many mistake for the "okay" sign, or even the pyramid hand sign showing allegiance to the global elite or Masons.

The levels of Monarch Programming identify the slave's "functions" and are named after the Electroencephalography (EEG) brainwaves associated with them.

Without a doubt, what Jeremiah reported are patented technological capabilities right down to intense high-tech sexual stimulation.

## Pulsative manipulation of nervous systems

**Patent number: 6091994**

**Abstract:** Method and apparatus for manipulating the nervous system by imparting subliminal pulsative cooling to the subject's skin at a frequency that is suitable for the excitation of a sensory resonance. At present, two major sensory resonances are known, with frequencies near 1/2 Hz and 2.4 Hz. The 1/2 Hz sensory resonance causes relaxation, sleepiness, ptosis of the eyelids, a tonic smile, a "knot" in the stomach, or sexual excitement, depending on the precise frequency used. The 2.4 Hz resonance causes the slowing of certain cortical activities, and is characterized by a large increase of the time needed to silently count backward from 100 to 60, with the eyes closed. The invention can be used by the general public for inducing relaxation, sleep, or sexual excitement, and clinically for the control and perhaps a treatment of tremors, seizures, and autonomic system disorders such as panic attacks.

Type: Grant

Filed: August 31, 1998

Date of Patent: July 18, 2000

Inventor: Hendricus G. Loos

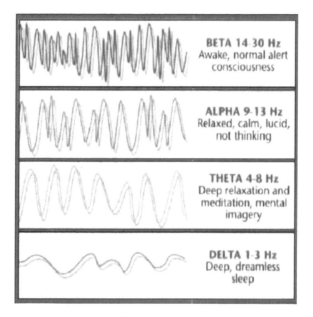

Types of brain waves in EEG

Regarded as "general" or regular programming, ALPHA programming is within the base control personality. It is characterized by extremely pronounced memory retention, along with substantially increased physical strength and visual acuity. Alpha programming is accomplished through deliberately subdividing the victim's personality which, in essence, causes a left brain-right brain division, allowing for a programmed union of left and right through neuron pathway stimulation.

BETA is referred to as "sexual" programming (slaves). This programming eliminates all learned moral convictions and stimulates the primitive instinct, devoid of inhibitions. "Cat" alters may come out at this level. Known as Kitten program-Ming, it is the most visible kind of programming as some female celebrities, models, actresses and singers have been subjected to this kind of programming. In popular culture, clothing with feline prints often denotes Kitten programming.

A T-shirt also seen worn by a popular entertainer today which sold out on the Urban Outfitters website said to be Illuminati connected.

If you Google: Project Monarch Sex Kitten Programming you will find several individuals in the entertainment industry wearing kitten type clothing which some believe, as stated has a definite connection to secret societies, Monarch Programming with the individuals becoming a Brand for revenue.

DELTA is known as "killer" programming and was originally developed for training special agents or elite soldiers (i.e. Delta Force, First Earth Battalion, Mossad, etc.) in covert operations. Optimal adrenal output and controlled aggression is evident. Subjects are devoid of fear and very systematic in carrying out their assignment. Self-destruct or suicide instructions are layered in at this level.

THETA – Considered to the "psychic" programming. Blood liners (those coming from multi-generational Satanic families) were determined to exhibit a greater propensity for having telepathic abilities than did non-bloodlines. Due to its evident limitations, however, various forms of electronic mind control systems were developed and introduced, namely, bio-medical human telemetry devices (brain implants), directed-energy lasers using microwaves and/or electromagnetics. It is reported these are used in conjunction with highly-advanced computers and sophisticated satellite tracking systems.

Jeremiah Ivie, is a bright, handsome, articulate man, who bravely mastered himself, in spite of his cruel targeting, and the attempt to manipulate him to murder through the unmistakable, powerful, capability to influence a person through electromagnetic radio waves, directly by the nervous system and the brain itself. Understand that this technology is no joke!

## Thermal excitation of sensory resonances

**Patent number: 5800481**

**Abstract:** In man, autonomic and cortical resonances of the nervous system can be excited by inducing subliminal heat pulses in the skin by means of a resistive heat patch, laser, heat lamp, or microwave radiation, or through a slow air jet that carries a small periodic fluctuation in temperature. Deeply subliminal skin temperature oscillations of frequency near $1/2$ Hz induced in a subject by any of these means cause sleepiness, drowsiness, relaxation, a tonic smile, ptosis of the eyelids, a tense feeling, sudden loose stool, or sexual excitement, depending on the precise pulse frequency used. For certain higher frequencies, the induced subliminal skin temperature oscillations cause fractured thought and a slowing of certain cortical processes. The method and apparatus can be used by the general public as an aid to relaxation, sleep, or arousal, and clinically for the control and perhaps treatment of tremors, seizures, and emotional disorders.

Type: Grant

Filed: December 28, 1995

Date of Patent: September 1, 1998

Inventor: Hendricus G. Loos

Jeremiah, joins a growing movement that will continue to try to bring awareness to horrendously personal plights of thousands, still enduring covert terrorism numerous untold reports of the similarity of ongoing human experimentation and tactics as a standard procedure.

He was told from inception that he was placed into a military technology testing program. This program factually originates within the Military Industrial Complex also known as the Department of Defense. Him being told this, from what I have learned, is the prevalent and typical arrogant insanity of those employed in these programs who essentially believe they are untouchable while playing God, although deceived by you know who.

Again, the power behind the secrecy is the belief today that it cannot be proven or in Jeremiah's case, that a victim would not be strong enough to resist the powerful stimulating urges, then expose what these operations are doing specifically to victims and the vicious plan for destruction of his family to isolate victims. Isolation is vital, away from family and friends by design which escalates the experiment without awareness of those close to the victim.

As I was told, "Someone gave us your name" in 2009 when my situation was taken to whole different level. The arrogance of these groups founded on the effectiveness of this technology's success with many others. Those involved with Jeremiah Ivie obviously felt that he would ultimately be controlled psychologically so they told him who they were at inception, believing he would do what they wanted through extreme beam torture, electromagnetic and subliminal influencing.

They must have believed they he would be unable to tell anyone, or if he did, definitely knowing that typically, no one would believe him, or perhaps even listen, and that people would think him seriously mentally ill especially if he revealed the level he was pushed to. As a result, they were willing to push him ruthlessly to the brink of disaster and destruction of not only his life but loved ones nudging him to hopefully murder, which historically has been typically backed up by strategic discrediting through covert, manufactured, synthetic mental illness labels which continue.

Today two acts are being used to cover up abuses of those targeted in these programs, and the denial of a U.S. citizen's rights under the Color of Law:

1.  The US Patriot Act, for example, protects governments and connected criminals from criticism and/or detection and prosecution. Under this act anyone whistleblowing or fighting the system on a major concern is arbitrarily deemed to be unpatriotic (when it's the criminals they criticize who betray us). They can then be listed (by a senior politician or at the request, through them, of a connected criminal) as a security risk and harassed covertly; using secret technologies.

2.  National Security Act of 1947 - The historic National Security Act of 1947 mandated a major reorganization of the foreign policy and military establishments of the U.S. Government. The act created many of the institutions that Presidents found useful when formulating and implementing foreign policy, including the National Security Council (NSC).

**Image -** President signing the National Security Act into Law

The Council itself included the President, Vice President, Secretary of State, Secretary of Defense, and other members (such as the Director of the Central Intelligence Agency), who met at the White House to discuss both long-term problems and more immediate national security crises. A small NSC staff was hired to coordinate foreign policy materials from other agencies for the President.

Beginning in 1953 the President's Assistant for National Security Affairs directed this staff. Each President has accorded the NSC with different degrees of importance and has given the NSC staff varying levels of autonomy and influence over other agencies such as the Departments of State and Defense. President Dwight D. Eisenhower, for example, used the NSC meetings to make key foreign policy decisions, while John F. Kennedy and Lyndon B. Johnson preferred to work more informally through trusted associates. Under President Richard M. Nixon, the NSC staff, then headed by Henry A. Kissinger, was transformed from a coordinating body into an organization that actively engaged in negotiations with foreign leaders and implementing the President's decisions. The NSC meetings themselves, however, were infrequent and merely confirmed decisions already agreed upon by Nixon and Kissinger.

The act also established the Central Intelligence Agency (CIA), which grew out of the World War II era as the Office of Strategic Services and small post-war intelligence organizations. The CIA served as the primary civilian intelligence-gathering organization in the government. Later, the Defense Intelligence Agency became the main military intelligence body. The 1947 law also caused far-reaching changes in the military establishment. The War Department and Navy Department merged into a single Department of Defense under the Secretary of Defense, who also directed the newly created Department of the Air Force. However, each of the three branches maintained their own service secretaries. In 1949 the act was amended to give the Secretary of Defense more power over the individual services and their secretaries, U.S. Department of State, and then Office of the Historian

The fact that this technology is 100% approved for legal use through DOD Regulation 5240.1.R specifically human experimentation by Procedure 13 is key.

### PROCEDURE 13 EXPERIMENTATION ON HUMAN SUBJECTS FOR INTELLIGENCE PURPOSES

A. APPLICABILITY

This procedure applies to experimentation on human subjects if such experimentation is conducted by or on behalf of a DoD intelligence component. This procedure does not apply to experimentation on animal subjects.

B. EXPLANATION OF UNDEFINED TERMS

1. Experimentation in this context means any research or testing activity involving human subjects that may expose such subjects to the possibility of permanent or temporary injury (including physical or psychological damage and damage to the reputation of such persons) beyond the risks of injury to which such subjects are ordinarily exposed in their daily lives.

2. Experimentation is conducted on behalf of a DoD intelligence component if it is conducted under contract to that component or to another DoD component for the benefit of the intelligence component or at the request of such a component regardless of the existence of a contractual relationship.

3. Human subjects in this context includes any person whether or not such person is a United States person.

C. PROCEDURES

1. Experimentation on human subjects conducted by or on behalf of a DoD intelligence component may be undertaken only with the informed consent of the subject, and in accordance with guidelines issued by the Department of Health and Human Services, setting out conditions that safeguard the welfare of such subjects.

2. DoD intelligence components may not engage in or contract for experimentation on human subjects without approval of the Secretary or Deputy Secretary of Defense, or the Secretary or Under Secretary of a Military Department, as appropriate.

"Exception Clause" of U.S. Code, Title 50, Chapter 32, Section 1520a for official testing by law enforcement and the military through the Department of Justice, Department of Defense, and Department of Homeland Security, and other highly placed government agencies, such as the, FBI, Secret Service, NSA, and CIA and now in full operation at also the State and local police levels should be eye opening. We are in the "Militarized Police State."

As shown, DOD Regulation 5240.1.R gives approval, as does EO 12333, and other laws, which appear designed so that those seeking information on who, what, where, are why, are well hidden by layers of secrecy and unethical approval. Through a combined organizational effort of involvement with many agencies, it is nearly impossible to get to the bottom of the dynamics of this program and thereby hold the individuals accountable for the extreme torture which would also result in shame and national disgrace.

In reality, the United States government, and other governments, has to be playing major roles for this type of program to be operating or exist on such a massive high level and unpublicized.

The laws and documented patented capabilities also continued to give definite credibility as a form of truth

Many have been beaten down, harassed, threatened and tortured into puppets, driven crazy, pushed over the edge, into complete submission, and compliance, using also death threats. It appears that victims that are able to withstand and rebuke the fear and torture have become worthy adversaries making the threats ineffective as a controlling source devised to stop publication and public exposure.

Disinformation campaigns have mobilized the community against the target through organized community stalking as an extension of the technological harassment. As a result, most are afraid to speak up, or possibly believe that they have done something wrong or, are, convinced they deserve this horrible, inhumane treatment in some way without human fairness or basic Human Rights. And those operating the technology appear to share this programmed belief which also makes it easy to terminate and destroy lives, limbs, and the pursuit of happiness not only in a target's life but also in the target's environment.

The amazing thing about murder is that once it is declared "okay or justified" by individuals or groups, or sanctioned by government agencies, or in this case, in the form of electromagnetic "slow kill" through debilitating one body part after the other, it appears that most having tasted blood, so to speak, have no consciousness about doing it again desensitized similar to Serial Killers.

Tim Rifat of the United Kingdom, documented the availability of the TETRA System, a system for mass mind control, by design and intent, to robotize police and the military personnel in "You Are Not My Big Brother."

History reveals that this technology, which first originated in the U.S. with one of the founding fathers of electromagnetic technology research, known as W. Ross Adey. W. Ross Adey later provided the technology, after perfection and to continue advancement to Great Britain.

Naturally, the author, Tim Rifat, The TETRA System: Mass UK Mind Control Technology and the Zombification Of Britain's Police is Now A Reality, who exposed its proposed use within the U.K., and globally by publication, as being technology designed to influence police to ruthlessly do to the bidding of the higher echelon through total police mental EEG entrainment, typically has been discredited in the media and everywhere else as a complete and utter fool with severe mental health issues and in need of psychiatric help.

Could mass control technology use on law enforcement and the military explain the levels of depravity some working in these programs appear to dwell or the lowest levels are willing to go? Or is it egotism, or the thrill and thriving on inhumane power to control another person's life, to include those having in most cases, more education than those operating the technology be a motivation as superiority? You do not need to be a Rocket Scientist to be employed to do this type of work. It involves, harassment, pushing buttons and beamed torture. No degree required.

One thing is certain, those at the top do not want known what is factually happening and these groups will go to great length to prevent exposure which includes murder if necessary to silence a whistleblower or any who has become a threat.

From my personal observance, there appears to be different levels to "The Program" and also different levels of torture or manipulation for specific purposes and statistical data. On a scale of 1 to 10, after reading Jeremiah's story, I would say he reached level 10 targeting years prior. When befriending him, I learned that his parent were world travelers creating games shows and he travelled with them assisting in creating the sets. The truth is they entire family could have been targeted without their knowledge, implanted and used as inadvertent spies by visiting so many places. If so, Jerimiah's targeting likely began to evolve in early childhood subtly and at some point, typical of this decade long program, in the victim's life explode as a full lab rat testing assault.

Being strong and secure enough to expose these extremely abusive and heinous acts performed on a target by those using this technology is mandatory and not a reflection of the target. It is a reflection of the powerful capability of this advanced technology to manipulate the human body and mind, and that those evolved are operating on the level closest the animal kingdom. For sport, or by assignment, as well as a reflection of the individuals doing outrageous, vicious and malicious things to other human beings while sitting comfortably at a mega computer connected terminal on their desks and never leaving the building.

Jeremiah Ivie, gaining my utmost respect later was also brave enough to report on Facebook information that as a form of ultimate, complete, and extreme humiliation to him, and anger by his Handlers, at their inability to continue to control him, that the technology was then used to humiliate him by making him defecate on himself during a date one night with a hopeful love interest.

Although I have not been caught this way yet, the technology has been used to repeatedly cook my bladder causing me to urinate on myself resulting in an immediate, powerful and uncontrollable urge to urinate immediately and the inability to hold my urine after the radar laser beam focuses on my bladder which materialized out of nowhere and without warning.

Other targets have reported that as soon as they urinate on themselves, five minutes later it happens again, as the bladder is completely drained through the beam holding its focused position. As a result of six times being caught this way; I learned that as soon as I feel the tiniest or minutest urge to get to the restroom right away. When they started doing this to me I barely could make it to a secluded area, such as the back of a business to hide in a parking area to urinate outside of my vehicle, much less try to walk into a restroom inside a restaurant or service station. Walking was completely out of the question.

Fortunately, I then took to sit on pillows to elevate me inside the car I had while driving which are washable in case of a beamed emergency. The patented creating loose stool was detailed earlier.

Oh, what great fun they are having doing these things to others. Once when I made it just in the nick of time to a restroom, one said, "Dang, I almost got her" as the drone follow me all over town, then the group erupted in laughter.

I personally can attest to having my bladder intentionally cooked while stuck in a fast food line sandwiched between vehicles, or when traveling on the freeway and the off ramp is miles away when going through the mountains heading home. This also includes while caught in traffic and being forced to urinate on myself as the beam tracks my movement around the clock.

Fortunately, I keep gym clothes in the car and have a universal gym membership and there are always one nearby, just in case.

The name of these games are extreme humiliation and torture, and degradation so intrusive designed to make you feel hopeless, give up, hurt yourself, or others, or to be committed to a mental hospital or jailed. And, depending on the circumstances, the ultimate result is covert technological murder.

Again, those working in these programs appear to be enjoying their power immensely as official sociopaths.

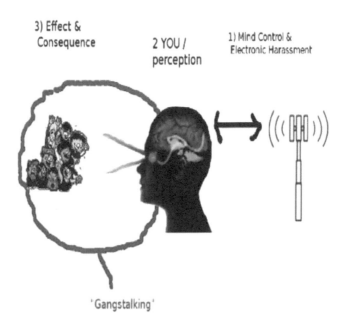

3) Effect &
Consequence

2 YOU /
perception

1) Mind Control &
Electronic Harassment

'Gangstalking'

U.S. Central Command Network Operations Center | Government & Military

Portable Drone Weapon System

# CHAPTER THREE
# Electromagnetic Sexual Stimulation

T he sexual theme is a common complaint among many targeted individuals. I myself have personally written several letters to federal, state and local officials complaining of the use of the technology in this manner on me. Because of this, it let up on to a certain degree, however, across the board, targets continue to complain of suffering unwanted electromagnetic sexual stimulation, both men and women, and likely even children by technology also having the capability to bring a person to a full orgasm. The patent and abstract of how it is done were detailed earlier exampled by Hendricus Loos.

During the weekend of early February of 2013, I had about five targeted individuals staying with me from Northern California for involvement for a protest and picketing of an event in Los Angeles to bring exposure to the targeting of many in California.

Major cities across the U.S. continue to be hotspots for technology testing obviously for a variety of specimens and California is major. While sharing horror stories about the use of this technology in our lives, specifically electromagnetic sexual stimulation continues to come up. One of the ladies in this group told me that she had an uncontrollable urge to masturbate, day after day and would. This was happening while being watched by men who are predominantly working in these operation centers. She also said that she was influenced into a lesbian relationship and that she is not gay nor was she attracted to women. To her, this was a wake-up call of the powerful ability of the influencing capability of this technology physically as well. She said that it taught her that she needed to be constantly in tune with herself, and her feelings, and fully grasp and understand what could happen to her, and more importantly, against her will if she were not by the operation around her.

It appears that operation center deviants are getting their kicks by creating their own personal versions of real time, reality porn.

Two women making out is probably a perk of the job, especially when they manifest the situation and likely a real source of mental masturbation enjoyment during their 8-hour shifts.

They tried to lean heavily on me as being gay or also having deviant sexual attractions or desires as well. This is common, and with some unaware, and of whom they want to control, for example, a politicians. This beamed capability assures a level of control of those in specific positions and also blackmail.

Jeremiah also mentioned this effort in his life regarding his loved ones and subliminal deviance of incest. Pedophilia thoughts are another topic reported by targeted individuals manifested through electromagnetic influence of these human monsters. The attempt to nudge people in this direction is just another example of the horror of the terrorism and how screwed up mentally and disgusting some of these sociopaths really are working in these programs and like in these positions for this reason. It really is sickening the level of filth formulated in the minds and character of some in these operation centers. It is as a direct result of their ability to tamper with the mind and emotions of a target. They are continually in search of, anyway or anything, they can use to get through to a target and control them emotionally and creating sexual deviance, again, is definitely high on the list.

The ability to create doubt within a person regarding their sexual identify is powerful and can impact a person's psyche deeply and even more powerful shatter the psyche by confusion of who you really are after these sensations. This is again why awareness is pivotal. Doing things against your will or against your belief system of which you cannot explain or agree with but do can be extremely shattering to the perception of who you really are.

Once a target succumbs to this type of influencing, those monitoring him or her, I believe step up the games believing victims have been successfully controlled, and have, at such a personal level, and they then can use you, abuse you, then berate victims, and tear you down. In other words, they are practicing amateur versions of Monarch Programming or Slave Programming and the proven effective dynamic.

A person falling into these traps opens the door to other areas of electromagnetic control when the manipulated target then hopes to please those handling him or her hoping for humane relief. In other words, they go in for the psychological kill with the sole purpose of complete and total control of a victim.

Because my only social activity where I lived by the summer of 2013, after moving outside of Los Angeles, California, is the gym or at home writing these books, the gym became the location where the technology was being used around me to influence unsuspecting people. The drone focus is on the victim, however, others around victims, can be influenced negatively.

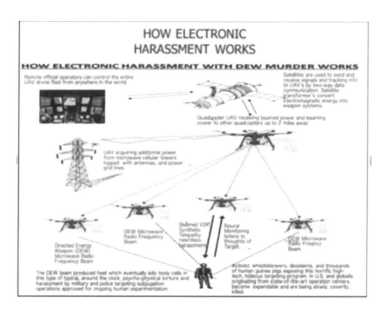

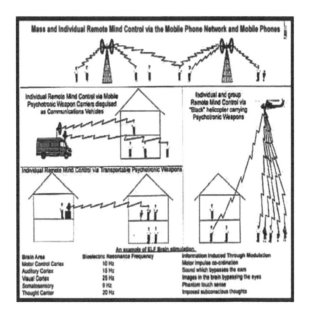

The objective is to motivate community organized stalking, or a community harassment effort of which many targets are familiar, and experience daily in their neighborhoods. This includes in their work environments of which usually cost them their job and livelihood. Homelessness is the name of the game ruthlessly by these operations. Some report community stalking as their only harassment which to me could indicate subtle subliminal influence which is typical. It can start out as harmless influence which grows to heinous influential thoughts as the testing continues to escalate.

When I moved, naturally the law of my jurisdiction, the Los Angeles Sheriff's Department, as was also in Arizona in 2009, were immediately notified and involved in the fused effort and this meant use of a powerful version of the portable microwave directed energy weapon pain ray beam documented as 100% being used by the Sheriff's Department nationwide and deployed from neighbor's residences with also military personnel reassigned at the helm for whistleblowers. Neighbors are on board as part of a nationwide community policing effort across America today motivated due to fear programming by the war on terrorism.

The problem is people were being deceived most times. I was not doing anything illegal inside my home, or out and it appears that in reality, I had been marked for death through toxic non-stop, non-ionizing radiation of which neighbors, may or may, not have known full well or understood the full potential of this technology as the beamed entered my home from surrounding houses.

My life had become a sick challenge to the egotism of this official group. I was not going to bend and they were determined that I would through both toxic and deadly torturous radio waves. There is no other outcome except illness due to a 24 hour a day, 7 days a week assault on a person, for months leading into years.

People being manipulated around me became easily recognizable for me because of my numerous experiences over the years. When the effort began to escalate at the gym in the ever-present effort to intimidate and frighten me, and create animosity and anger towards me from perfect strangers, I was not surprised and was prepared. In fact, I expected it from past experiences.

One day a young man got into the hot tub and appeared just too happy to see me and greeted me as if we had met before or were old friends. This perfect stranger asked me how I was doing; I replied "Well." He then replied, "You are still alive?" I replied, without forethought, "Alive and kicking." He then immediately got out of the hot tub and left for about 15 minutes to meet up with whoever sent him I realized set-up in the men's locker room. When he returned, I decided to question him about exactly what his comment meant. Naturally he had no idea what I was talking about. As we talked, I explained to him the dynamic of the typical harassment scenario within the targeted community of stalking of which he already knew and was more than likely a part of hoping to feel him out.

Under normal circumstances someone making a comment about life or death, in this manner around me would hold no specific meaning or it would possibly be funny perhaps. However, if your life is being constantly threatened around the clock, you take notice if someone out of the blue, and a perfect stranger, said something like this to you. The perfect crime would be to create random assassinations of trouble makers appearing to be motivated by one of their mentally controlled patsies. As we continued to chat, I was not surprised when he told me that he and his wife are targeted individuals too. Many are promised their freedom if they join "The Program."

After this revelation, he then admitted to being very angry and bitter about what is happening in his life as a result of it and also to his family. Later when his wife got into the hot tub with us, she mentioned the FBI distinctly while in a conversation with another person who had also gotten into the hot tub with us, then intentionally look directly at me. I assume hoping for a reaction. There was none.

I have observed several times, the strategic use of targets against targets within the targeted individual community. Why not make a target useful if you are already monitoring them anyway?

Targeted individuals may also have a unique dedication to their handlers through a desperate hope for the torture to cease and become loyal and thereby easier to control to include a motivating small stipend. They probably may have been told also, as I had, that if I worked with them, they would leave me alone. And because people are being viciously attacked, covertly and secretly with no recourse, legally, or otherwise, it appears plausible that many jump ship. It is the old adage, "If you can't beat them, join them."

However, remember, once in this program it usually is for a lifetime as mentioned by Harlan Girard, during the Jesse Ventura episode "Brain Invaders" episode. He, now elderly, reported during the show that he is still fighting the battle for his life and sanity after nearly 30 years of technological telepathy and electronic harassment. He stated during the interview that he believed that he had been initially placed into "The Program," after making what was perceived as a derogatory comment about George Bush senior years ago.

I believe that people are in these programs indefinitely because, logically they have to continue to monitor you and to keep tabs on you and that victims become a part of their handler's list of targets of which they are responsible for monitoring. They learn every aspect of your personality. For example, if you are hot-tempered, they know what could push your button and use it. It is also very easy to connect with any target, or anyone for that matter, by a body scan, then by simply typing a name into the computer and the target be located anyplace on the globe within a matter of seconds as mentioned by satellite. First and far most, the goal is to break the target down and to gain control. If the target resists, it appears that they become a much-sought challenge to test the technology in many areas to include dream manipulation. This also could be possibly the reason why some have been in these types of program for decades.

A well-known whistleblower, interviewed on the Coast to Coast Electronic Harassment episode stated that he had been told, by an insider that about 300,000 targeted individuals within the United States have not been successfully controlled by this technology. He also expressed his grave concern that this figure would indicate that the rest of society have successfully been and now operate in a Hive Mind by Artificial Intelligence.

For targeted individuals, in reality the promise of relief is merely another facet of a psychological operation or PsyOps and a characteristic of this program's overall effort to keep the target in conflicting emotions and in confusion, the primary goal.

I had observed other targets around me not as sincere as they were portraying themselves to be also during the visit by the group from Northern California for the protest. One of the ladies, as soon as she arrived, wanted to immediately zero in on how my situation evolved saying we needed to talk because it was exactly identical to hers. I was unsure at first, and gave her the benefit of the doubt. However, when she began calling me every day after she returned home, wanting to stay on the phone for hours, it appeared that her intent was to sacrifice me for her life and for relief from the torture being inflicted on her and her family. She said they had begun targeting her son at pre-teen age and he was diagnosed as psychotic as a result. He was then medicated before she became aware what was really happening.

On another occasion, a shady looking guy followed me around, menacingly, as I moved from the sauna, steam room, then to the hot-tub on two separate occasions at the gym trying to frighten me. I had remembered to put my books in my back pack, after noticing the escalated effort there to influence people. I also created business cards to pass out to people, with my website, blogs, and Amazon Author's Page. When I pulled them out and started discussing the books with a regular at the gym, I observed this guy listening intently. After he heard and saw the books and listened to me talking, he then got up and left. They began to use regulars at the gym that they saw me conversing with, who all appeared to have a meeting with someone in the men's locker room after our conversations. I found it amusing that the locker room was the headquarters.

I can only imagine what people were being told. I had no doubt that I was mentally unstable of which I had heard before from someone. One day, in hope to incite a negative reaction from me by gym staff, a Sheriff followed me from a store near the gym, and then before I entered the gym, went in before me, briefly, said something to the customer service people at the counter, then left. When I came in I noticed a decisive change from the typical cordial greeting I usually got. It was a look from one of the desk clerks of me possibly being a crazy. Again, these are joint targeting fusing of personnel and over and covert technological efforts. He could have been telling them to keep watch on me for this reason or possibly just playing a role.

The combined effort is to plant rumors or disinformation of the target being something that they are not to include gay, a pedophile, a drug addict, a criminal, prostitute, child abuses, mentally disturbed, etc., etc., etc., then people treat you badly as part of the psychological operation.

In my case, repetitious compliments of me being attractive or "I like that girl" were also said in games, with another replying, "She's cute," all day long, on and on and on, as a strategic ploy. I assume I was supposed to think they liked me as they continued the covert physical torture around the clock.

For their amusement, they would heat my body with the directed energy weapon to such a high level that I had to take off my shirt and sit around in my bra as I worked on my laptop writing this book dripping with sweat profusely. I once even heard one of them say, right before heating me, "I need to see some tits."

The relentless compliments appear to be said more from the standpoint and hope to implant or brainwash me that I should be mesmerized, interested and fascinated by one of them and invite one of these vile creatures into my life because he likes me although again, they are torturing me around the clock and deteriorating and slowly killing my body. In my case they desperately wanted to get next to me, make no mistake about it, because of these books with a definite hope to neutralize me anyway they could. I was also asked to work with them because I am supposed to be so intelligent or smart. In reality, I am just doing what I am supposed to be doing and that is stepping up to the plate and rightfully fighting for my life, the lives of my loved ones, and anyone I can help along the way. And, as I have documented, I believe exposure is the only way.

In May, I had my car with a handsome repairman who kind of liked me and whom I thought was cute. As I sat on the driver's side of my vehicle, he worked under my steering column connecting a loose wire. He declared that he did in fact like me but his penis might be too small for me. I did not have to ask him where this thought came from. We never had any conversation even remotely close to this subject before and he was out of line. It likely was a beamed thought that just came up out of the blue. I looked at him amused.

Knowing the capability of the technology and seeing with my own eyes, after eight years, the games, and how it is being used, to manipulate and to keep love interest away from a target, I knew that those watching me around the clock, were more than likely beaming into his head. I advanced out of the animal kingdom in another lifetime and am not and have never been motivated by primal sexual urges. I am stimulated by something other, and more valuable than sex from a man, such as intelligence, compassion, humor and strength of character.

When he said this out of left field, it was not difficult for me to figure where this thought likely originated in his mind. He probably while working and thinking that he liked me, while they listened deciphering his thoughts with the brainwave scanner, beamed into his head that he did not have a chance with me because his body part was too small which also could be used create useful jealousy and resentment.

This was not the first time I had dealt with this subject from the men in the operation center. Needing yard work done, I hired some workers from Home Depot. For example, I am very selective to pick those who were older and looked harmless. However, while in the house, cleaning while they worked, I was being beamed, rape, repeatedly from the corner house behind mine set as the nucleus of what is happening around me.

I looked out the patio door to see how well the two were progressing. I witnessed a totally different demeanor and change of character by the returned stare. I also without a doubt saw a bulge in one of their pants which was an erection.

On another occasion while at the gym, a midget body builder appeared extremely angry at me when I watched his wife whenever they came around. She had a lot of tattoos and I just was fascinated by a women body builder in such good shape after three small children. I was not sexually interested in her at all or women period.

However, apparently this thought was beamed into her husband's head it seemed. One day, he sent her over to stand next to me to see what my reaction would be or if I would try to flirt with her or talk to her it appeared. She just stood right next to me waiting for me to say something to her. When I ignored her; she then left and went back over to where he stood waiting.

After I realized was had just happened, I became upset a little. After they both left, I vowed that the next time that I saw them; I would broach the subject just to see if I were right. As it turned out, I was. I struck up a conversation with him another day then told him about technology in use today which can beam the suggestions of people working in state-of-the-art operation centers directly into your head to influence you I said.

At first, he must have immediately thought I was crazy and began to laugh until I said, for example, they might even beam a suggestion into a person's head that I am gay, and want their wife, when I totally am not gay and do not. When I said this he immediately changed, the smile was instantly wiped off his face and I could tell he looked at me in a different light due to what I suspected by the stunt previously likely being true.

Still working within the lesbian theme, in late July of 2013, a young woman showed up at the gym, I later realized with the explicit intent to get next to me for an operation center show. This was after many of the men they sent had tried and failed. I did not recognize it until later, that this woman was involved. As I sat in my favorite location, the hot tub, she eased her way slowly closer and closer to me.

This woman appeared to be an okay person and did not seem gay and was dressed in a feminine swimsuit I thought later as I drove home. Some, who are decisively gay, at times wear more masculine looking clothing. It was another lady who struck up the initial conversation with me at first which opened the door for this person to become involved in our conversation.

As we talked, I later realized that she had expertly drawn me in by literally quoting every chapter of the new book I was working on at the time, a metaphysical book called "The Heart is Another Name for God – Lotus Dream" to appear as if we randomly had something in common. Oddly, it seemed that this small inspiration, metaphysical book, disturbed the group around me most of all.

This probably was because it showed my ability to focus on another subject which again made questionable my being insane. At first, I thought that we held the same interests and metaphysical beliefs of which I write about in this book; however, later I realized that she had been likely coached and it was probably happening while she sat talking with me that night in the hot tub by those watching and listening from the operation center. After getting out of the hot tub and seeing her in her regular clothes, later in the women's locker room, she was dressed in man attire that indicated that she was 100% gay and down for putting on a show for her deviant Handlers.

In the hot tub she had first started talking about fear, then expertly switched to ego, and almost verbatim quoted similar information in each chapter of this book. She also asked, to further draw me in, for help with a book she hoped to write, sounding just like mine, of which she said she was trying to publish. Later as we headed out of the gym at the same time to our vehicles she asked me out, in what sounded like a request for date. When I told her, I wanted to invite a friend of mine who likes country music along with us, if I decided to go, she became anxious, immediately got an attitude and left. Going to the gym at least three times a week, I never awe hide or hair of her again.

Later that night, after detailing the situation to the friend I wanted to invite with us to the Darius Rucker concert over the phone, I heard those monitoring the call then say, say, "Don't send her" meaning the woman, "around her again."

As the effort began to center around me at my only social location, it appeared that quite a few people, actually about ten people at the gym were either being used or playing along as the hopeful organized-stalking effort continued to play out and manifest. While sitting in the hot tub alone, the tub began to fill up with men obviously involved as I calmly sat watching them one by one, one day. After three of them got in and did not look at me, the fourth, a white male got in. When I said, "Well, well, well, it looks like the gang is all here," the white guy immediately got out and left, and two others exited the hot tub shortly thereafter.

They refuse to accept that I am not scared and will not allow myself to be intimidated and more importantly appear to be in complete denial that their constant and repeated effort to implant and manipulate fear, verbally and subliminally, has failed them and the only thing it has gotten them are now three books on the subject after a thorough education for me of the mechanics of their operation by them by actions.

After the other three left, I then tore into the last one, who had tried to ingratiate himself with me on two separate occasions by conveniently showing up at the gym, at the odd times I am there, believing himself fascinating, and trying his hardest to start up a conversation with me by acting like we were buddies. He later asked me how I knew who they were while not admitting he was one of them.

By August of 2013, after moving in August of 2012, to the neighborhood where I lived at that time, the operation was set up in houses, both front and back, on both sides, and angular to my home insuring monitoring and technology deployment from every angle from these residences with portable, see through the walls real time infrared vision. I began to get hit by many methods and from many directions to include from the operation center itself through drones or the method they believed effect from moment to moment, to include, satellite delivered or communication towers. As early as May of 2013, I counted a least seven to eight houses being used around me.

A characteristic of these operations, I had learned is moving around from house to house so that you cannot pinpoint the location of the beam origination from one specific location. Operatives want to get up close to the target, to make the target deathly ill faster being so close.

The real neighbor and homeowner of one of the houses directly next door to me, it appeared 100% allowed a couple to move into their home and pretend to be them. I later met the real homeowner at the post boxes, seven months after I moved in one day, whom I had never seen before at all. I questioned her about the other people staying in her home and she did not, of course, know what I was talking about until I asked if she or any of the neighbors would deny involvement before a federal judge. The look on her face was a classic Kodak moment. The expression was that of complete surprise that I was aware of what was happening, or that I had figured it out, and then an immediate extreme cautious look then followed and a vain attempt to convince me that she did not know what I was talking about again. As I got back into my vehicle, I said, "If you say so" then one of the men in the operation center, typically observing everything said, "I can guarantee they are all going to say, we don't know what she is talking about." And later, one of these men verbalized something that is common knowledge and pretty consistent in covert technological harassment targeting, "Nobody is going to believe you anyway!"

In "You Are Not My Big Brother" I document major funding for these programs and these highly technical targeting appear to be well funded in "The Program" with money to spare to test handheld, portable, land, sea, and space-based technology and lease locations and pay for use of residences around victims as an incentive.

This neighbor told me she had been on vacation when I told her I had never seen her before having to fess up. Although she was in fact the real homeowner, someone else obviously pretending to be her, and even driving her vehicle, a common tactic, had been monitoring me from their home with the technology and had burned my large spot off the top of my hair.

Another neighbor, who lived directly next door to the elderly gentleman on the opposite side of me, where the beam was deployed due to the location perfectly situated to my bedroom for all night long head cooking inadvertently told me that the elderly gentleman's wife had told her "That some people are after you" meaning me one day as she watered her lawn and we chatted.

I was driving a rental truck with my car in the shop for repairs. It was too big to fit into my garage. The next day, when I was leaving, I noticed the molding had been pulled off the brand new 2013 Silverado. Many targets know this as part of the typical mobilized harassment and destruction of property effort in neighborhoods where hate and anger are directed at a target motivated by the originating agency.

By 2013 I had been single for seven years as the men targeting me intentionally destroyed possible love interests, and repeatedly told me, "we are not going to allow anyone around you" or because of the around the clock monitoring of me since early 2006, when i did meet people, "we are going to ruin that too" as they desperately hoped to affect me and control every aspect of my life. And they did destroy all relationships.

I was also told, after they listened to my natural desire for a relationship by e.g. thought deciphering one day, that if i dated one of them then they would leave me alone. My response to this was "sure, when you give me back two healthy hips, destroyed by the repeated microwave directed energy weapon focused attacks" which eventually required two total hip replacements one in 2017 and the other in 2017. I had held off on the second surgery as long as i could.

On August 27, 2013, the well-known whistleblower previously mentioned was the guest on Coast to Coast and interviewed by George Nory, the show title was "Electronic Harassment." During this interview, the subject of many women being primary targets in these programs was mentioned. I personally was surprised when he stated that it is typical human nature for the predominantly men working in these programs to target women as even possible love interest. I had issue with this statement although he was absolutely right, but because it was unethical, immoral and unscrupulous.

The whistleblower then went on to explain how he became proactive. He revealed it was after his ex-fiancé was targeted, watched around the clock, inside and outside of her home, then those targeting her entered her home and raped her after putting date rape medication into a favorite drink in her refrigerator.

Unfortunately, the men working these programs are allowed to watch people, in real-time, when bathing, undressing, and dressing each day and apparently are ill equipped to handle this excitement as dangerous idiots. And why are predominantly men working these programs anyway? This probably is due to unethical behavior in these centers of which women in the environment would find unacceptable, offensive or even protest.

The shows advertisement reads:

In the first half of the program, the whistleblower discussed his work with thousands of victims of electronic harassment, stalking, and mind control. Based on his research, he noted various kinds of electronic harassment, including being stalked by mysterious forces and, chillingly, "attempts at controlling the mind." Additionally, he said, victims report "hearing the voices of perpetrators in your head that you only can hear, while you are being attacked with directed energy weapons."

He theorized that this ongoing electronic harassment is part of an overarching experiments to ultimately find the technology which would allow for control over the entire global population.

While political dissidents are potential victims of electronic harassment, the whistleblower suggested that middle to lower middle-class people as well as prisoners and the homeless could also be seen as ideal candidates for testing the technology.

He explained that this would allow for those who are controlling the experiment to get a greater data set and see which tactics work best. However, the whistleblower also put forward a troubling potential alternative scenario which was imparted to him by an insider working with this technology. According to that source, the whistleblower said, the victims of electronic harassment are actually the outliers who are not susceptible to the control system. "That's a very scary thought," he observed, "because that tells me that the majority of people are already being controlled…"

During this timeframe, those around me were in an ongoing, constant, and lively debate, in the operation center about whether I am attractive or not. It would appear that some of these men, sitting around in these state-of-the-art operation centers, have nothing to do except torture or judge within the psychotic herd pack a woman's physical attributes. Heaven help the women they perceive as being attractive or intelligent. Their apparent weak minds, combined with their constant involvement with the woman or in this case women, every day, and around the clock, nonstop, appears to then result in an emotional attachment by these sickos.

It is no wonder that some in Senate are reporting, that these fusion and police counter-terrorism centers have become useless wastes of time, energy and resources. There simply are not a lot of terrorist within the United States, compared with the two to three Counter-terrorism division that have evolved, and have in turn turned the technology in use today on activist, whistleblowers, on dissidents labelled as "Domestic Terrorist" to include high-tech drone beamed torture.

The only thing that curtailed the unwanted sexual stimulation with me was these non-human humans not wanting anyone to know the levels of depravity or their perverse enjoyment of essentially electromagnetically molesting a woman for kicks. As I have written detailed in "You Are Not My Big Brother," I was told that some women, women like the electromagnetic sexual stimulation, however, I was not one of them as they had hoped. If you ask me, there is no excuse for these men targeting women they, in reality, would never have a chance to get next to any other way, or under normal circumstances. And when all else fails, from my personal experience, these sadistic non-human humans easily turn to vicious name calling and crippling torture.

In this battle, I had already decided that they would have to kill me before I submitted to these creatures, albeit they are clean shaven, and in neatly pressed uniforms, or suited in clever disguise of what they truly do for a living. I am sure their appearances and the prevalent programmed mentality about themselves as authority figures, or being for the people, and to serve and protect, serves to distract people from the capability of some capable of horrendous abuse and a chance to play out the inherent evil and deviances lurking within secretly making them little more than official criminals.

Due to my awareness, and experience, of how this technology can and is being used, I became familiar with it, and watched as people I met, looked off into space, in a brief trance and I watched repeatedly their expressions change to a look of experiencing possibly the synthetic telepathy software at that moment from the operation center. The look is a look of listening to thoughts, similar to when we temporarily become oblivious to our surroundings briefly while thinking, and then return back to the moment. Part of the documented brilliance of this technology is also the capability to expertly mimic the targeted individual's voice which is documented in the abstract for the Neurophone patent, invented by Patrick Flanagan in 1958. This is the first version generally believed to be delivered via satellites.

This technology is advancing very, very fast today. It is documented that the voice mimicking capability was used in operation desert storm on Iraqi generals using voice transformation software to mimic other generals. Perhaps what is most interesting and perplexing of all is the fact that, many other countries know that the united states has and is using psychological electronic technology, but amazingly it is little known within America itself and obviously by direct intent to keep it hush. The "Voice of God" "voice of Satan" or "voice of Allah" is being reported as the reason for creating horrific atrocities documented by a brilliant activist and creator of ominsense.org as shown.

"Dalton told us that literally, when he logged onto [Uber's app], it started making him be like a puppet," the police documents said.

He claimed that the devil head "would give you an assignment, and it would literally take over your whole body."

Killer driver told cops the devil possessed him through Uber app

Arman Torosyan, 23, killed his parents – 64-year-old Khachik Torosyan and 57-year-old Marietta Torosyan in their apartment in Sevan, as he says, "fulfilling the commandment of Jehovah."

**Source:**

"When I stepped in, I felt compelled by a higher power," Hammer told the Orange County Register. "Honestly, have you ever been grabbed by the Lord in a way you never thought you would or you could? That's exactly what I'm testifying to, and I'm not speaking in hyperbole. I'm speaking right from the heart."

_Teacher Says 'Higher Power' Told Him to Attack Kid on Skateboard_

Police in Richland Township, Pa. say a 26-year-old man killed his grandmother while she ate breakfast, then claimed the Archangel Michael told him to do it.

*Levi Daniel Staver Allegedly Stabs Grandmother Connie Johnston, Blames Archangel Michael*

The boy was found not guilty of murder and wounding with intent to murder due to a troubled mental state that led him to embrace Satanism. The court was told the boy had notebooks full of "meditations" on the afterlife and had – on at least three separate occasions – heard what he thought to be the devil's voice.

*Teen Who Claimed Satan told him to Kill his Parents*

On Monday, 27-year-old Ayanie Hasan Ali casually strolled into a recruiting center in Toronto and began stabbing two members of the Canadian military while shouting "Allah told me to do this, Allah told me to come here and kill people." Ali is a Muslim and a citizen of Canada. Police have leveled multiple charges against the attacker, including attempted murder.

*"Allah Told Me to Come Here and Kill People" Declares Muslim Man While Stabbing Canadian Soldiers*

The nanny accused of beheading a four-year-old girl in Moscow and waving her severed head outside a Metro station told journalists before a court hearing that 'Allah ordered' her to murder the child.

*'Allah Ordered Me' to Kill Child*

Files said Laney believed that God had told her the world was going to end and "she had to get her house in order," which included killing her children.

*Attorney: Woman thought God told her to kill sons*

Jennifer told investigators a "spirit" voice told her to harm the baby as a test of faith, according to court documents. "She said she knew that it was wrong to harm the baby, but that the `spirit' voice assured her that the baby would be returned from the dead," the documents state. "Just like Jesus raised Lazarus, I threw the baby on the stones by the pool," she told investigators.

*Mom: God Told Me to Kill My Baby*

However, The Root reports that Williams was a non-practicing Jehovah's Witness at the time of his death. Yet one thing seems certain: given the fact that Williams claimed that God told him to kill WDBJ journalists, it seems self-evident that Williams believed he was doing the will of God.

*Virginia Gunman Claims God Told Him to Kill WDBJ Journalists*

A woman who allegedly stabbed her husband said she did it after, "Jesus and Mary told me to kill him because he is Satan's spawn!" according to a police report.

*Suspect: "Jesus And Mary Told Me to Kill Him Because He Is Satan's Spawn!"*

She allegedly added, however, that "Jesus" had told her to drown her son. Police also say she claimed that her son had "become stuck to the ground."

*Victoria Soliz Allegedly Tries to Drown Son in Puddle Because Jesus Told Her To*

What makes this case relevant here is that police indicate that McCuin told them that his god, presumably the Christian god, made him kill Shearer.

*Accused Murderer Says God Made Him Kill*

Tejada told investigators God told her to push a rose in the girl's throat to exorcise the devil.

*Mother who 'murdered daughter after God told her she was possessed by the devil' is found NOT guilty because of mental illness*

(RNS) A New Jersey man who claimed God made him kill his pregnant girlfriend will get a new trial because jurors deciding his case should have been allowed to hear special instructions about an insanity defense, an appellate panel has ruled.

*"Man, Who Says God Told Him to Kill Girlfriend Gets New Trial"*

The accused killer of Carlos Castro will argue that he believed he was acting on instructions from God when he murdered and dismembered the 65-year-old Portuguese TV personality and gay activist in a Manhattan hotel last year.

*God Made Me Do It Defense in 2011 Midtown Murder*

"God told me to do this. God told me to cut off children's heads and bring them to him and then I would be made king," stated Drissa Coulibaly after being caught hacking at two young boys with a machete in Yopougon, a suburb of Abidjan.

*'God told me to cut off children's heads and bring them to him…': Ivory Coast children kidnapped and brutally butchered in suspected ritual killings*

"I didn't enjoy killing at all. I said sorry, but the son of God was controlling me."

*Matthew de Grood Systematically Stabbed 5 people to Death*

In an email, he sent at 11:19 p.m., he wrote: "I've been getting hit with the direct energy weapon in my chest all evening. It hurts really bad right now." Police say he opened fire on campus about an hour later.

*Myron May; "I do not want to die in vain." – NBCNews.com*

Because of the capability to mimic your voice or that of another person, a thought or a suggestion can appear to be your very own because it is strategically in your voice. This, makes it very difficult to explain to someone or convince them what could be factually happening to them after some nonsensical thought materializes in their head or worse. This is because what is being said sounds as if victims are thinking it when in reality, they are thoughts being beamed.

Microwave technologies carry this capability as do portable technology and specific types of computers and laptops having weapons system software installed are capable methods also such as the Panasonic "tough book" laptop shown in the image previously.

With me as Jeremiah Ivie reported, the beam was repeatedly attacking area where there is little skin to bone such as even my neck. I can hear the bones cracking when just turning my head slightly as I sit here now with my back to the house behind where the beam seems to be originating.

I thought they had worn out their welcome in the houses they initially set the torture technology up in on my block but later realized that perhaps they had trained neighbors on its use which is not uncommon. Without a doubt, USAF is heavily involved and as I passed a corner house one day, an air force uniform came out and waved at me twice in sync with my leaving from the corner, four houses away.

They were determined to get something out of the deal and I am determined that "I am not lunch." My response to assisting them in any way, "sure when hell freezes over." I don't make deals with the spirit of the d-evil nor do I have to negotiate with them at all. I'll take my chances faithfully to God.

The individuals working in these programs exhibit classic psychopath personalities. They complement, manipulate and stimulate sexually, then torture. A psychopath is not happy unless manipulating someone. They sit in these operation centers and appear to take great pride in nudging people, into hurting themselves or others as puppet masters energized by their person demons and deviances. They destroy families, lives and relationships by creating chaos through beaming suggestions into any environment, to include jealousy for motivation.

How would you characterize men, sitting in an operation threatening to destroy your family member's life? How would you describe men who refused to leave still believing in the capability of the technology to ultimately gain control of people, alter consciousness and manipulate a target into heinous acts? How would you describe men, who after the effort failed, and exposure looms overhead, began to show their true colors, as subhuman individuals who will kill inconspicuously?

From what rock did these lowly individuals crawl from under that would motivate them to want to, or even consider destroying the life of a young woman, my daughter, because they could not use her to get through to her mother? And, on top of this, what if they are simply playing out their TETRA programming by their leaders as robotized minions who are convinced via their indoctrination that what they are doing is somehow honorable in their blindness or powerlessness to stop.

Who is really sitting at the computer motivating such unbelievably cruelty?

This 6,000-year-old artifact of a craft hovering above, a helmet on the person's his head, an antenna tower between he and the craft, while holding an object appearing to deploy a focused beam on two figures being electromagnetic drawn to him.

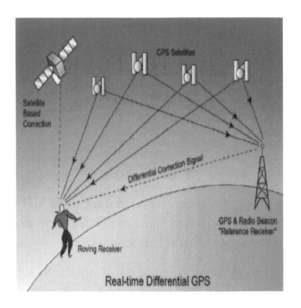

Example of satellite / craft hovering, connecting rays to tower antennae resulting in GPS bio-coded, biometric (DNA, iris, gait, facial or voice recognition), human tracking from a state-of-the-art operation center capable of deploying coercive, physical-psychologically manipulating RF technology.

# CHAPTER FOUR
# Slow Kill

N ot only are people suffering in the United States, but activist all over the world continue to join forces to do whatever we can to expose what is happening to us.

Many thanks to Peter Mooring of the Netherlands for the accuracy of his numerous websites, and his excellence in detailing the Slow Kill System and specific areas of focus of the ELF beam, in the following graph which details covert technological torture areas of focus with is literally everywhere on the victim's body.

As I stated, this is a unified, his graph depicts the torture many endure thoroughly, and of which is being reported, again, as identical by targets all over the world and a Standard Operating Procedure.

Electronic torture, Electromagnetic torture, Microwave torture, Electronic murder, Electromagnetic murder, Microwave murder, Organized murder, cooked alive, Electronic mind control, Electronic mind reading, Brain zapping, People zapper by Peter Mooring, Netherlands

## A GLOBAL REIGN OF TERROR

Peter asks that you make a copy of this graph, go to the websites, and watch the You Tube videos! I join him in asking that you spread the knowledge!

July 12, 2012: New! STOPEG forum, contact others, exchange information, etc.

This website is the home of the following domains (I registered these domains to make sure they will not be used to prevent exposure of these horrible crimes):

[Mar 31, 2013] Survivors on Military Targeted Kill List presented evidence of being slowly killed while used for barbaric, cruel and unusual, torturous research, to Senator Ron Wyden of Oregon. A Targeted Killing advocacy group presented documentation of the United States intelligence community applying covert slow-kill methods to silence victims while using them for research in American communities.

## Wyden Letter 2/11/13 - CANR Non-consensual

Kill List Targets Used for Barbaric Research, Evidenced with Sen. Wyden, by Deborah Dupre (March 20, 2013)

Microwave Torture, War Crime Against Targeted Individuals and Inmates, by Deborah Dupre, Human Rights Examiner (September 10, 2010) excerpt: there have been such powerful (electronic) weapons that can be used to monitor, incapacitate, torture and murder, all without evidence. The ones owning and exploiting this technology will rule the world if we do not stop them, not tomorrow but NOW. ~ Peter Mooring, Human Rights Reporter

## Excerpt:

Los Angeles County Jail is to be first of U.S. prisons to use the Assault Intervention Device (A.I.D.), a 7 ½ foot tall military grade weapon to microwave inmates, what Los Angeles Truth Movement head, Chuck Noyes identifies as a war crime. This is one of many new weapons that can be used to torture and kill Americans in Obama's authorized targeted killings of Americans program. (See: Directed Energy Weapons aimed at American targets: Learning opportunity, Examiner)

**NOTE:** Many inmates were innocent and still victimized.

**In another excerpt:**

"While this "Pain Ray" device was being tested by the Air Force, a mis-calibration of its power settings caused five airmen in its path to suffer lasting burns, including one whose injuries were so severe that he was airlifted to an off-base burn treatment center.

"It is all the more disturbing that the use of the Pain Ray is being entrusted to the deputies of L.A. County Jail, with its long-troubled history of deputy violence, retaliation and abuse against inmates.

The ray gun shoots blasts of heat energy at prisoners that penetrate beneath the skin to the pain receptacles reports Times News Feed.

ACLU attorney told Associated Press that the device is "a weapon that can cause serious injury that is being put into a place where there is a long history of abuse of prisoners."

**On September 2, 2010, Dupré reported:**

"Since the 2001 September 11 attacks and Bush's so-called "war on terror," there was a soar in number of Targeted Individuals reporting covert assaults by black operatives, thugs, extremist cells, "stalkers." Some TIs are reporting assaults with remotely applied, military grade, lethal weaponry. These reports have been from both overseas and U.S. self-identified targets. In early August, Sharon Weinberger explained the reason for the escalated reports:

"After the attacks of September 11, the Pentagon began a shift away from its late Cold War–era 'two-war strategy,' premised on maintaining the ability to conduct two major military operations simultaneously, and began to focus instead on "irregular warfare against individuals and groups." (Emphasis added; Sharon Weinberger, Black Ops: Secret Military Technology in the Age of Terrorism, August 3, 2010)"

# Do you want others to read your thoughts?

Do you want others to push a button to make you burp, sneeze, cough, scratch, fart, urinate, control you sexually, give headache, cook you alive, etc., through the wall in your home with invisible laser weapons? Do you want others to force thoughts into your brain?

All of this is possible and done illegally today! But your government does not tell you anything!

Electronic weapons are one of the best kept secrets in the world. All over the world thousands of innocent people are attacked and manipulated, incapacitated, tortured and murdered with these weapons most of them never knowing what happened. Read all about this and tell your family and friends. Peter-Mooring

**Electronic harassment and electronic torture list, February 26, 2009**

**The people cooker – cooking people like a microwave oven cooks meat**

**What is electronic harassment/electronic torture/electronic murder?**

Electronic harassment/electronic torture/electronic murder is about harassment, torture and murder using electronic weapons based on radio waves. These weapons have been very refined over the last years and can cause effects comparable to many illnesses and/or injuries. These weapons are not science-fiction but used today illegally by your national secret services on mostly random innocent victims not knowing what is being done to them.

Update Sep 3, 2011: Mark Rich, known for his website www. The Hidden Evil. Com. put up his new site this week with much more background information www. New World War. Org.

Update Sep 10, 2011: Must read for targets and people who are seeking the truth…

The Ultimate Blasphemy: The mechanism of covert mind control reading and other high-tech crimes

If you want to read about symptoms then check the article below Electronic harassment and electronic torture list.

If you do not know much about electronic harassment, electronic torture, electronic murder then you may want to start reading:

- The people cookers – cooking people like a microwave cooks meat.

- Military COINTELPRO targeted killings lawsuit spotlights American civilians by Deborah Dupre on September 2nd, 2010

- Collateral Damage USA: Extremist cells target 350,000 U.S. civilians by Deborah Dupre on August 30, 2010

- ZAP! Have You Been Targeted by a 'Directed Energy Weapon'? Victims of Organized 'Gang Stalking" Say it's happening in the USA (article by Victor Livingston)

- Synthetic Telepathy and psycho-electronic weapon attacks on hundreds of thousands of innocent U.S. citizens by a combined 100,000 FBI and NSA "Psychopathic Secret Society Spies in America" or

- **Google:** Brigitte Althof victim story

- Tortured-www Guantanamo. Com

If you want to read more check the links on this page:

http:// www. Electronic torture. com/links.html

If you want to read more, including gang stalking (organized stalking):

- Electronic weapons already control our lives!

- Secret Service: Fear for the truth to be revealed! (11)

- electronic weapons arrangers and operators burn people, burn children, burn babies

- Torture and murder without evidence (2) educate yourself

- Electronic torture / electronic weapons: people burners and people cookers (speed cookers)

**Check the electronic harassment and electronic torture… list… below**

<u>**Peter-Mooring**</u>

### What is electronic mind control / electronic mind reading / brain zapping / synthetic telepathy / remote-neural-monitoring

Electronic mind control is about forcing thoughts into your brain using invisible radio waves (this can be done from long ranges). Your attackers can make you think about a certain person at a certain moment, force a song into your brain (so you will start humming/singing it). Your attackers can also make you stand up and walk to your kitchen. If you do not know about this then you will be just following the thoughts that were planted into your brain. In other words: you are robotized.

Electronic mind reading is about reading your thoughts using invisible radio waves (this can be done from long ranges). Already it has become 'easy' to decode received brain signals into words spoken to oneself without talking. At the moment, they also make progress with decoding images from what you look at (as seen by you through your eyes)

This is not science-fiction but done today illegally by your national secret services on mostly random innocent victims not knowing what is being done to them.

**If you want to read more:**

Warning you no longer can trust your own thoughts

Secret Service: Mind rape targets to steal, torture, murder, create enemies, (and call them terrorist) or here:

Secret Service: Electronic Mind Control, Electronic weapons used on people surrounding the target WITHOUT them knowing this or here:

Brain zapping by Jason Jeffrey or here:

## SYNTHETIC TELEPATHY AND PSYCHOTRONICS

Electronic weapon attacks on hundreds of thousands of innocent us citizens by a combined 100,000 FBI and NSA psychopathic secret society spies in America, or google:

- Remote Neural Monitoring

- Recent documents about mind reading:

- Mind Reading: Technology Turns Thought into Action – Joe Hamilton (May 12, 2011)

- Mind Reading Experiment Reconstructs Movies in Our Mind – Associated Press (Published September 22, 2011

- We're closer to mind reading than you may think – Emi Kolawole (October 31, 2012)

- Can a Satellite Read Your Thoughts? – Physics

**Revealed**

Stalking, electronic torture, shooting with directed energy…weapons…from…the…sky:

A video and two victims reporting the horrible details like many other victims, they can only conclude that the attacks also are coming from military aircraft. From comments accompanying video:

— Microwave weaponry systems like the Active Denial System are used in tandem to deliver physical attacks designed to stress targets, torture them physically, and turn their homes into places of extreme distress. Hoping to drive the target from their-home, -or-workplaces.

**From:** Electromagnetic Warfare, letter by Carolyn Williams Palit

— The pain is unbelievable. It involves tones, harmonics, hissing, stabs, blows, voice to skull transmissions, induced dreams (nightmares), burning sensations in the body and head, internal burning sensations inside of the body and head, crawling sensations on the body (phantom touch), electronic rape, induced and unwanted urination or orgasms, holographic inserts, and many other horrible tortures. My thoughts seem to be scanned every-second.

**From:** webpage about next victims of electronic "mind Control" torture:

— (Carolyn Palit) I thought I was dying. I thought that I would spontaneously combust into flames. Either it came from a base in the hills, or Commander Solo*, or it came from the heavens.

— It attacked…me…for…two…years.

**From:** webpage Carolyn Palit talking to Jesus Mendoza

— Some of his attacks are coming from the direction of the houses of the defendants that he has named in a law suit against these kinds of attacks. But . . . mostly . . . the attacks come from "straight up." -

## More information about electronic weapons attacks, including mind control and mind reading

On the STOPEG.com website, there is a CBS News video of the Active Denial System (ADS), a microwave laser weapon. Although the DOD wants us to believe this is a safe weapon (that is why they showed it to us), experts agree it is not! This video shows a big installation, but there are many kinds of laser weapons. Some are very big and mounted in trucks, ships, aircraft, or even in satellites. But there are also much smaller, portable versions, that can be very-effective.

Of course, military and secret services have equipment based on the most advanced technology available. Their equipment is not available to the public. But now advanced commercial devices are being shown on the internet giving an idea of how easy it must be for the attackers to cook, burn (torture) a person. One is a portable (hand-held) laser, the S3 Spyder III Arctic laser. Although it may appear not very sophisticated, imagine someone pointing this at your back when you are in a restaurant or at the movies. To look at people through wall take a look at the XAVER 400 Compact, Tactical Through-Wall-Imaging-System.

Many targets wonder how they can be attacked so easily when they move to a different location, e.g. a family member, friend, or go to a hotel. The attackers stuff their portable laser weapons and through-wall imaging devices into their suitcases, book rooms close to yours, and often will attack you from two different angles to confuse you. In case you prevent them to attack the body area they want to attack, e.g. by putting your back against an outside wall of the hotel, they call in military aircraft that will blast you with very high-power microwave (HPM) bursts, cooking your inside. (This happened several times to me, last time on July 6, 2011, while staying in a hotel in Westkapelle,

Netherlands, the aircraft arriving around 1 a.m. about 15 minutes after they concluded they could not perform the attacks on my back).

Many people have a problem thinking that others can read their mind, their thoughts. Again, the advanced technology used by military and secret services is not available to the public, but today more and more commercial devices are becoming available. One company delivering a mind reading headset is Emotive, for USD 299, -. With this device, you can control your games, your TV set, etc. with you mind! They also have an API (programming interface) to create your own mind reading application.

I cannot emphasize enough that not all but many attacks are from the sky. When driving your car, they may burn your back (from the sky or from some equipment in your own car) when another car is driving behind you and make it go away when the car goes away. If they do this every time then you probably will think it has to do with the car behind you. When driving your car, walking outside, riding your bike, they may burn your head and make many people you look at scratch their head. Sometimes people are part of the sick network but many others may just have been beamed the same way you are, having no clue about what is going on (your attackers want you to attack other people, they don't care about anything because they are psychopaths, murderers and child abusers.)

Another warning is for a much more confusing type of attack: electronic mind control. In this case your attackers will plant thoughts into the brain of people surrounding you. Of course, these thoughts relate to your life in one way or the other. They may even plant your (!) thoughts into the heads of people surrounding you. If you do not know about this then you may start to think that these people can read your mind, which can be very depressing. I wrote several articles about electronic mind control, if you are a target and do not know about these capabilities, you may want to read this.

- Links, portable laser weapon, portable through-wall vision, mind reading headset, voice-to-skull:

- The S3 Spyder III Arctic

- XAVER 400 Compact, Tactical Through Wall Imaging System

- A do it yourself blue laser from DVD reader

- Emotive, mind reading headset and APIhe Swi MP3 waterproof MP3 player, underwater sound without ear buds, using bone conduction

## Hearing Voices

If you are hearing voices you may be a mental case but it is also possible that you are a target of (highly illegal) mind control activities by some sick bastards. In your country secret services including military are developing weapons that make you hear voices and covertly testing these weapons on random human beings or groups of people. Some terms used to describe this phenomenon:

- Voice-to-skull

- Microwave hearing

- Silent sound

Perhaps the easiest (and cheap) way to attack a person this way is by the Audio Spotlight. This device makes you hear words etc. spoken by someone, but the persons around you do not hear this. Check the links below for more information:

1. Microwave auditory effect (Wikipedia)

2. Hearing Microwaves: The Microwave Auditory Phenomenon by James C. Lin

3. Microwave hearing by Mark Rich

4. Sound from Ultrasound (Wikipedia)

5. Audio Spotlight (Holosonic company website)

6. Hearing voices = Voice to Skull (Cliff Huylebroeck website)

You Tube video on Audio Spotlight, Sub vocal Speech and Microwave hearing (one of the many videos on this subject)

SWIMP3, underwater MP3 player without earplugs

Electronic harassment and electronic torture list - February 26, 2009 - Updated December 24, 2009

[Published: February 26, 2009. Updated: February 28, 2009, April 11, 2009, June 10, 2009, June 13, 2009, June 25, 2009, September 6, 2009, December 24, 2009]

Almost anybody can become a (temporary) target of these horrible electronic weapons. Please read what can be done so you are prepared. This is not science fiction but happening right now in our 'democratic' society.

Below is a list of all possible attacks by electronic weapons that I know of by experience. I know more attacks exist. Female targets write about sexual attacks, others mention continuous ringing in the ears, etc. I may add these later. I decided to keep this list personal, i.e. in this blog I write down only what has/is being done to me, not what is being done to others.

**Electronic weapons**

These attacks are done by the following kind of electronic weapons:

- Directed Energy Weapons (laser weapons), like ELF (very low frequency), ultrasonic, lasers, (high power) microwave weapons

- Through-wall vision

- (Sub-vocal) Mind-reading

- Microwave hearing/Silent Sound (letting you hear sounds/things in other ways then hearing by the ear)

For another introduction, you may want to read:

**The people cookers -** Cooking people like a microwave oven cooks meat. or, read the summary of my previous blogs:

**Secret Service:** Fear for the truth to be revealed (24) – Gang Stalkers and people cookers are murderers, the crimes they commit belong to the worst crimes in history – Part 2

## A list including all horrible details

On the internet, already a lot of symptoms and attacks by these weapons can be found. Most of these lists do not detail these attacks and that is exactly what I am trying to do here. In my opinion, it is not enough to read that such a weapon gives you a burning feeling, instead the horrible details must be exposed!

**Description of a (continuous) high intensity microwave weapon attack:**

This weapon makes your skin really burn like a very heavy sunburn and cooks your inside, you really feel yourself being cooked alive, and you are heated like meat in a microwave oven, with intensities that exceed those of a microwave oven. Gall is coming out of your throat and fluids inside your body evaporate making you instantly burp. In case of high intensity there is also a burning sensation on the other side of the body, where the beam, of approx. 10-30 cm diameter leaves the body.

If they cook you long enough cooked body cells explode inside you, when aimed at your upper body, lung cells explode/ are destroyed and reducing lung capacity immediately noticed when walking stairs or running. The burning sensation and the cooked-inside feeling will go away after 5-30 minutes or 1-2 days depending on the duration and intensity, it may take a day or more to recover from high power microwave bursts with durations of 5-60 seconds (but can you recover from these amounts of irradiation?). A cup of milk is heated and starts evaporating after 5-10 seconds. The electronic weapons aimed at you can make you burp or fart within 1-3 seconds; hence the intensity of electromagnetic irradiation is not only used to torture a person but murder as well.

## Covert and intended-to-notice (or noticed) electronic harassment/torture

Electronic harassment is called covert if the target does not know about these weapons and methods. If you do not know about these weapons you may think you have all the bad luck in the world, you will wonder what strange things are happening to you, to your body, and accept you do not control your life anymore.

If intended-to-notice (or noticed), electronic harassment is torture in its most horrible form. What would you do if your body is made to react every time to events occurring in your life, e.g. by making you burp or fart, your legs are cooked every night, your ankle is cooked during daytime when working behind your computer, your knee is beamed to cause maximum pain, etc.

### Some examples

To delay you:

- They make you go the toilet to urinate when you want to leave your house

- They cook your legs before running

- They burn and cook your body high power to prevent you doing you work

Note that this delaying is often done together with gang stalking methods like cars blocking your road, phone calls when you are to leave your home, etc.

To make things worse:

- They make you sneeze extra times when you have a cold

- They cook your throat become sore when you have a cold

- They attack your eyes until red with blood

- The cook your legs after running

- They cook or burn where you have pain already

To torture you:

- They cook and burn your body everywhere

- They cook your family, your children, friends,

Note that this torture is often done together with gang stalking methods like synchronizing saw machines, honking horns of cars, screaming birds (pigeons, crows), etc.

## The maximum pain business, beyond imagination horror and cruelty without evidence

Special methods have been developed to make you think you have a heart problem, erection problem, toothache, etc. For the ones exposing these horrendous crimes they developed methods to inflict maximum pain, e.g. by cooking such a person alive with a high-power microwave weapon, or burning the skin of the target or making the target burp or fart every few minutes to events occurring in the life of the target (including e.g. opening a website on a computer, saving a file, cars passing by the window, etc.). Some authors refer to the development and use of these weapons as the pain business. I would like to make a correction, please call it the maximum pain business.

After accepting that there are really such sick and disgusting creatures actually developing and applying these methods and torture, you also have to accept that it is not about just pressing a button, but also about the way how this torture is applied. Zapping your eyes red to make you look bad, cooking biceps to prevent you from swimming, cooking your throat to prevent you from singing, inducing heart problems and toothaches to prevent you working or sports. More horror, these methods and procedures could not have been highly developed without being tested on humans, on real persons. And again, more horror, these methods are often used with gang stalking (organized stalking) methods. Like they cook your ankle with insane intensities making your foot very painful, and when you go outside all kinds of people with leg problems are crossing your path, people limping, in a wheelchair, sometimes even someone without a leg. Or, they start sawing wood somewhere and when the saw enters the wood cook your body with high intensity-microwave.

This torture is applied 24/7, not once every hour but more like once every minute/every 5 minutes. Horrible torture that can be called torturing a person to death.

**Special case: The heart attack**

Damaging your body can be done in several ways. One vital organ is the heart. They can attack the heart very effective with:

- Microwave weapons, cooking the heart area slowly

- High Power Microwave (HPM) weapons, cooking the heart area in a second

- Ultrasonic weapons, pressurizing the heart area

- Heart frequency manipulation weapons

These weapons can damage your heart in a split second; you may not survive such an attack, but can also be used to slowly damage your heart. Slowly cook your heart area so you will get a strange feeling and in fact your heart is really damaged. Then there is also the frequency manipulation attack, your heart may feel pulsing, blobbing like crazy.

Cook heart area from the front, often together with a cook beam from left behind. Slow damage, horrible feeling

Flash your heart with very high-powered microwave. Instant damage.

Pressurize your chest, even takes your breath away if applied with enough power

## Pulsate your body/heart area with low frequencies

These effects will give you a very realistic heart attack or heart problem feeling. Your heart may start pounding very loud, may feel very painful, the heart area may feel strange, cooked. If applied with enough power, this really damages your heart and heart area. Your heart is cooked like meat in a microwave oven.

Can you recover from these attacks? In general, they will not murder you or leave evidence, your heart may feel very painful for several days after they stop their attacks. It can take weeks until all pain in the area has disappeared. I am not sure about permanent damage caused by these attacks.

Can you die from such an attack? Yes, if the intensity of the beam is high enough your heart can be damaged or temporarily disturbed in such a way that you will die.

How can you recognize a 'normal' heart problem from an 'induced' heart problem? You yourself are the best judge of what you feel. If you believe something really is wrong with your heart then visit a doctor. If you are certain your heart is attacked then avoid visiting a doctor as this will confirm a heart problem in case you collapse or die, case closed.

If your heart is under attack you may receive strange emails like the one below:

## Radiofrequency Radiation Dosimetry Handbook - Chapter 2

Dear XXXXX,

Well I'm still alive at this moment, but I think they are trying to give me a heart attack. Anyone with a radio can use this method and cause damage to any organ specifically. The FCC has really fallen down on the job. Basically, any mob can do this to you. And I do believe the FBI and CIA and NSA are mobs. They take out contracts and are evil and stupid.

The woman who now heads our safety department said we could not bring spectrum analyzers to work. I do not think anyone but me would have understood what that is. What this means is that we are not allowed to protect ourselves, as if these evil doughy people should be our judge jury and executioner.

The Nazis used this technology in WWII. that's how old it is, maybe older. they are still using it along with MRI'S and infrared through the wall. their favorite thing to say is, "you can't prove it." which, of course, proves it.

XXXXX

No one is free if one is not free.

## Impossible to protect yourself

The human body appears to be extremely vulnerable to electromagnetic irradiation of all kind of frequencies. The human body also is an electromagnetic transmitter and sensitive (radio) equipment can pick up and decode the signals that are generated e.g. when speaking, thinking. In contrast to a knife or a bullet, electromagnetic signals are not blocked by walls, compare your cell phone. Limited protection is possible using sheet metal, metal plates, water, vacuum, but if you really are a target the attackers increase intensities (if necessary to insane levels), change frequency, attack from different angles etc. Also remember that these weapons can hit a person without hitting the person sitting next to this person. They can be aimed and the diameter of the beam can be made small enough to hit only the target.

## Anybody can be a target

Electronic weapons make it very easy to eliminate persons, to get persons (temporarily) out of the way, to murder persons, etc. all without evidence, and most of the time even the target does not know he is zapped, cooked, burned with electronic weapons. The ones owning and controlling this technology now can get everything they want in a very easy way. They can get their football player into the national team by temporarily cut out the competitor for the same position in the team. This could be done with other means as well but it is very easy with electronic weapons. Just cook a person's ankle and foot during the night and the damage is done. To influence a tennis match, you could cook a player by heating the body with microwaves (compare microwave oven). He will just feel overheated and sick and lose the game.

These are just two examples to demonstrate what can be done. You can imagine almost anybody can become a target. Some people because they are more visible then others, because they have something the sick network wants, because they know something the sick network does not want to be exposed, because they are too intelligent for the sick network, just for personal reasons because maybe they made a remark about someone, etc.

**Electronic weapons can kill a person**

Besides using electronic weapons to monitor, drive into suicide, cause temporary injuries, they can also be used to kill a person. Killing is possible by sending wrong signals to the heart making it pulse in abnormal ways, or by increasing intensity and cooking the heart area, damaging the heart slowly. Very high-power laser weapons or HPM (= High Power Microwave) weapons can damage your heart-in-a-second.

Although little is known at this time about the effects of long-term irradiation, it is not difficult to imagine that this will cause all kinds of diseases as electromagnetic irradiation destroys your DNA (cell with damaged DNA are called cancer). Again, all these horrible things can be done, and are done today, without evidence.

How do you know you are a target of electronic harassment?

It is often very difficult to distinguish between normal body behavior and induced body behavior if there no signs of burning or cooking. E.g. would you know the difference between normal diarrhea and induced diarrhea? Yes, you are able to decide what is not normal by comparing your diarrhea with previous experiences. It may start and disappear very sudden, may cause other effects like water bubbles leaving your anus, etc. Also, the diarrhea may be linked to a certain event, like picking up your child, appearance in court, etc.

Always ask yourself what it is you are feeling did you feel this before? Does it go away when you turn your body 180 degrees? Does it go away when you walk in the streets or drive your car? You are the best judge of what you are feeling.

**Your car may be tagged**

When you are a target you will experience harassment everywhere every time. If you have a car they will tag your car (these are words I learned from a 'so-called target'). This means they will equip your car with electronic weapons not only to monitor you but also to cook and/or burn your body while driving.

They may also harass the target covert and use the following beams:

- Sleep beam, to make the driver very sleepy

- Eye beam, slowly cooking they eyes, so tears come out and visibility reduces

- Just to confirm, all this is done to cause the (mental or physical) death of the target.

- Harassment from (neighbor) houses, cars, handbags, airplanes, satellites

Most of the electronic harassment comes from close neighbor houses. When you walk in the streets you are probably attacked by electronic weapons (directed energy weapons) from houses (they may be remote controlled or controlled by operator at these locations. If there are no locations for their equipment, they use these weapons from their cars. You may also be hit from airplanes. This is not difficult to believe if you accept a reach several hundreds of meters. Some targets write about satellites being the source of their electronic harassment. In general, I do not believe this is true.

Example of current state-of-technology:

You can be hit by very accurate equipment. e.g., when you are running on the streets or in the woods you may be 'shot' with a very high-power microwave weapon in your calf from an airplane. The intensity can be such that this causes instant injury. Your calf is cooked within a split second and your muscles almost instantly tear apart. Making running/walking almost impossible.

Electronic harassment can also be done from small devices carried in e.g. shopping bags in shops or on the street. You need only a small battery to give the target a single burst that makes him burp or fart. This is enough to depress the target: nowhere safe from this horrible harassment.

Satellites probably play a big role in exchanging information about a target, e.g. you can have a sub-vocal speech decoding PC in the house next to target, but it is easier (and safe) to transfer the un-decoded information to a central computer system, and return the decoded words. But it may be done on site; PC's have enough power today to do this decoding themselves.

You may be attacked by persons (family, friends, co-workers) who are covertly attacked by electronic harassment

The aim of the attackers is to drive the target insane. To speed up things they aim their electronic weapons covertly at family, friends, co-workers, etc. to make them react in several ways to what the target is, doing or saying.

Some (easy) methods used to covertly attack other persons:

- Scratch beam, to make a person scratch his head

- Sneeze beam, to make a person sneeze

- Cough beam, to make a person cough

- Urge to urinate beam, to make a person go to the toilet

**Examples:**

They beam persons around the target on the head so everywhere around the target people are scratching their heads

They beam the target's head very hard and then beam the head of a friend so that this friend will start scratching his head immediately very visible for the target to see

When the target and partner are in the same, then every time the target opens a website on his PC (not visible for the partner), they beam the throat of the partner causing the partner to cough almost immediately

When the target is beamed in the stomach during work, they make a co-worker sneeze at the same time

When the target is beamed in the stomach, they beam her child in the stomach as well, making the child cry and saying it has stomach pain (this is confirmed by multiple victims)

Once again illegal and (beyond imagination) horrible crimes by our national secret services.

## Elite and secret services control our politicians

It is not amazing that these weapons exist, I studied computer science myself, and if you have enough money it is not that special. It is also not amazing that there are actually sick and disgusting creatures walking around free applying this kind of electronic harassment to cause the physical or mental death of a person.

What is amazing is that a lot of high ranked politicians and other influential persons are fully aware of the existence and use of these weapons but do not speak out. What does this say about these persons? I believe you can say that the idea we live in a democracy has disappeared completely.

Elite and secret services are trapped by their crimes in vicious circle of more violence against the people of the world

The ones facilitating, outsourcing and performing this cruel electronic harassment and torture is not just a group of people, these attacks are very well designed and applied by people trained to cause maximum pain but leave no evidence. The ones I am referring to are our secret services, including military. They are tightening their grip on society, not because they have to protect us against the terrorists in the world, but because they are getting more and more afraid what will happen when the truth about them is exposed. They are trapped in some sort of vicious circle. To maintain themselves they must commit more and more horrible crimes. And to avoid their crimes are exposed they have to perform new horrible crimes, etc. etc.

So here we have the elite, creating wars to maintain themselves, and their armies, the secret services both trapped in their own lies and deceit. And the horror for us, the people of the world is that we will be taken from (created) threat to (created) war because that is the only way out for the (criminal) elite and (criminal) secret services.

**People cookers and secret services**

I introduced the word people cookers in 2007 for the creatures facilitating, outsourcing, performing electronic harassment and electronic torture. Main reason is of course that people cooking comes closest to what they are doing. Most of the harassment and torture is done by microwave irradiation which causes heating of the skin and your inside just like a microwave oven cooks meat. There are no words to justify these illegal and horrendous crimes. The ones involved are disgusting creatures, an author called them 'the failed human beings' and that is just what they are. They were born human, choose the wrong path in life and degenerated into pieces of shit.

I believe people cooking and gang stalking (organized stalking) are the perfect example of how sick our national secret services have become. They now commit the perfect murder, in their language meaning murder without evidence. And they now steal, torture and murder just because it has become so easy to steal, torture and murder.

# Electronic harassment and electronic torture list - December 24, 2009

Below is the list of all (most) effects I experienced from these horrible electronic weapons. Few times I may not correctly describe the source of the effects. It is sometimes difficult to point to microwave or ultrasound. Both can be very damaging. High Power Microwave cooks your body cells while high power ultrasound simply destroys your body cells. But in the end the result is the same, a damaged body.

### ***MIND-READING***

Sub-vocal speech        Special equipment is used to

Detect muscle contractions like the one a person uses when speaking out loud. When spoken to itself these muscle movements can be detected by advanced equipment and translated into words and sentences. As most people talk to themselves when 'thinking' this resembles mind reading.

### How it is applied

They read your sub-vocal speech and react to it

### Feeling

Unbelievable at first, then you get depressed because the last thing

you thought was private appears not to be private anymore. Then you accept that you probably are even more popular and watched then the big stars in the world and sometimes use it to deceive the bastards.

Horrible torture

**Why it is applied**

To drive you insane

Seeing through your eyes

Although some targets claim that they can see what you see. I have not (yet) experienced this. But they do everything to suggest that they can do this. e.g., on the highway you are burs with the burp beam every time a favorite model car passes in the opposite direction.

They are looking at you from some camera builds inside your car or from another car. They are looking at your eyes to see what you are looking at.

I experienced a few times I was burst. BEFORE I saw the favorite car. A lot of research in this area is going on, I will keep you updated.

## **HEARING VOICES** -

Voice-to-skull  Special advanced equipment is used to beam voices, or in fact any sound, into your head.

**How it is applied**

They make you hear voices that you should not hear. For example,

they let you hear voices from people far away very clear as if they are standing next to you. This an amazing experience. There is a lot of reports of people who claim they are attacked by voices

**Why it is applied:**

To drive you insane

### ***HEAD***

## Top of your head beam

The top of your head is very sensitive. They will burn the top with some laser or microwave weapon

## How it is applied

They put the beam on your head and wait for you to move

Feeling can be very painful if applied with enough intensity. You cannot do much with this beam on your head.

Horrible torture

## After effects

If applied with high intensity it may take several days for the painful feeling to disappear

## Why it is applied

Prevent you from working, doing your thing

## Should you worry

Yes, long term irradiation may cause brain damage, tumors

## Scratch beam

They just beam your head some-where. The normal reaction is your will start scratching your head.

### How it is applied

Mostly applied when other people can see you. If they do this every time with the same people they may wonder what's wrong with you. They also apply this and have random people scratch their heads and then burn you feeling

Not very painful, mostly a short pulse, although they may keep the beam on your head and remove it after you start scratching your head

### Why it is applied

Drive you out of your mind, drive you into attacking other people

## Headache beam

This beam gives you a headache. It is some kind of high intensity low frequency beam. The headache appears suddenly and also disappears suddenly

### Feeling

Can be very painful

Sickness/Alcohol beam

The feeling is that you feel a little bit dizzy, see thing a little foggy.

### How it is applied

They may apply this when you drink your first glass of beer, wine, etc., or when you have a cold, or are sensitive to hay fever

## Heat Cooking

They put the microwave beamer on your head and your head is heated. They may do this after you drink a glass of wine, but also after you turn on the central heating of your apartment. You will feel hot, sick, slow.

## Ear short burst

Your ear is burst, the idea is to hit your eardrum. With your eardrum cooked/damaged you have a strange feeling. Ear continuous beam. Your ear is beamed for very long time just to present you pain, they want you to move.

## Feeling

It appears your eardrum and surrounding area is very sensitive. This is very painful.

## Eye blur

Your eye is burst and you have instant blurred vision. Often your eye will start tearing

## How it is applied

Some kind of microwave burst,

See also Phasr and other similar military weapons used to blind the enemy

## Feeling

Not really painful but you cannot do much as you are used to two eyes.

**Why it is applied**

Prevent you from working

Should you worry

Yes, this is very damaging for your eyes

## Eye sting

Your eye is burst with some kind of laser beam

**Feeling**

Like they drive a needle into your eye. Very painful

**Why it is applied**

Stress and discomfort

Just below eye, tremble

They beam at the area below your eye and the flesh below it starts trembling. They can do this in shops and through wall

## Burn (beard) hair

They burn away hair at certain locations, e.g., your moustache hair just below your nose holes to create the illusion of a leaking nose

**How it is applied**

This is just a laser hair removal procedure, like performed in many beauty parlors

## Sneeze burst

You are burst and must sneeze. This is a tingling sensation that can makes you sneeze in an instant

### How it is applied

You can turn your head in the other direction or hold your hand before your nose to make sure the attack is caused by electronic weapons

### Why it is applied

To make your body react to something

## Runny nose

You have a runny nose but do not have a cold. You may start thinking you have some kind of strange cold but you have not. Once you are out of the beam, the runny nose disappears.

### How it is applied

I am not sure if this is done only by electronic weapon or by a combination of some drug and electronic weapon

## Cough burst

Your throat is burst with a high intensity burst and you start coughing instantly. This coughing does not look like normal coughing

You will have a sore throat immediately afterwards.

## Dry cough

Like something fluid/moisture sticks in your lungs, or sometimes your throat. When you breathe you hear/feel a rasping sound. You must cough very hard to throw it out.

## Toothache

Using a low frequency beam, they induce a toothache, this really is a horrible feeling. It is like a true toothache but now when you move out of the beam it disappears.

### Why it is applied

Prevent you from doing anything, just plain torture

## Sore throat

Your throat is slowly cooked and you will almost immediately notice less volume and after some time pain while speaking

### How it is applied

They can do this in just one or two hours by aiming a high-power beam at your throat.

### Why it is applied

Prevent you from speaking loud, prevent you from singing

## Blackout beam

This is very high intensity burst on your head. There is no pain but it feels like the result having been hit on the head very hard. You feel a bit dizzy and your ears are ringing

### ***UPPER BODY***

On top of shoulder

A very painful beam on the top of your shoulder

**Why it is applied**

Just torture

## Cook chest/lungs

I call this beam: through-body-beam. You are really cooked by this beam. If applied with enough intensity you will feel a burning sensation on the back (where it enters), then feel the beam cook your inside, then you start burping, then you feel a burning sensation on the other part of your body where the beam leaves your body

**How it is applied**

This beam can be applied everywhere, from the house next to yours, from cars. When they beam you outside the intensity often is higher as they want to make sure you are hit properly

**Feeling**

You feel like being microwaved.

## Very painful, horrible torture cooking

They put the microwave beamer on your body for a long time and you have the feeling you are cooked alive which in effect is a very accurate description of what is being done

**Feeling**

You feel like being cooked alive, horrible torture

## Burp beam

This is a low power sophisticated version of the chest/lungs cook beam. It is difficult to locate the source direction.

**How it is applied**

It takes approx. 2-3 seconds to make you burp, make your body react to events. They also may apply low intensity, so you get an irresistible urge to burp but cannot

**Feeling**

Horrible torture

**Why it is applied**

To make you suffer. This applied sometimes once every five minutes, but sometimes also several times a minute to let your body react to events like cars passing your window, etc.

Horrible torture.

## Heart attack incl. extra beam from left behind

This is a low frequency high power beam aimed at your heart, mostly from a position somewhere in front of you. To maximize the effect, they simultaneously beam you from the left behind position with a microwave cook beam.

**How it is applied**

As they may apply the from behind beam for a long period. Your flesh around the heart area may get cooked and the whole area may feel painful and stiff

**Feeling**

This really gives you the feeling of having a heart problem, and in fact you have! The difference is that this one is applied by murderers.

Horrible torture

After: It may take several days before you recover (if they stop the beam)

**Should you worry?**

Yes, your heart is vital

**Heart attack high power burst**

This is a very high-power burst of very short duration, 1 second or less, that will give you immediately an extremely painful heart (area). This beam is really amazing: I believe it can kill you in an instant

**How it is applied**

They can do this through wall anytime

**Feeling**

Horrible torture

**After effects**

It may take several days before your body recovers and it all feels normal again

**Should you worry**

Yes, your heart is vital

## Heart attack blobbing feeling, heart pulsing strangely, randomly

This may be done separate from other heart attacks. Your heart may start feel pulsing funny, the feeling is very massive, it also feels like bubbling, like the heart lost control of normal operation and just pulses somewhat

**How it is applied**

Not only frightening but also very painful

## Pressure beam

They put a pressure beam on your chest this will take your breath away and you may think you're are having a heart problem. This can have various intensities

## Back burning

They burn the skin of your back. This can be low intensity or high intensity. The feeling is you have a sun burn, in case of high intensities it will also color your back a little red.

**How it is applied**

This almost instant skin cooking.

Refer to ADS (Active Denial System) for details

**Why it is applied**

Present pain. To move you out of the way, to make you leave the swimming pool, etc.

**Electric shower**

This is an overwhelming effect.

This is like a shower but not with water but with electronic pulses.

**Heating**

The temperature of your body is increased giving you the feeling you have a flu or some kind of illness.

**Spleen beam**

Beaming in your side gives you the idea you have spleen pain

**How it is applied**

They often do this during high intensity sport activities. The idea is to make you believe you have real spleen pain and will stop your exercise

### ***ARMS***

## Biceps

They cook your biceps to reduce their power, make them feel painful when you load them during e.g., swimming. This may be done to prevent you from doing your sports.

## Muscle weakening in hand

They beam your hands. The result is that you cannot hold a pen between thumb and finger like you used to, also you cannot put your fingers against each other (like making a cup with your hand).

They may do this to prevent you from working or doing your sports e.g., swimming.

### ***LOWER BODY***

## Stomach cooking

They put a beam on your stomach and the stomach begins to bubblelike something is cooking inside.

## How it is applied

They often do this at night.

## Should you worry

Yes, long term irradiation may cause stomach cancer, tumors

### Kidney damage

With some kind of ultrasound beam they attack your kidneys. The feeling is like you have been kicked over and over in your sides. This is like the feeling that is described by patients that have their kidney stones crushed by ultrasound.

Intestines cooking, urge to defecate

They cook your intestines and you feel you have to fart but cannot.

### Fart beam

They cook your intestines and it will start bubbling. After some time, you will have to fart

### Blind gut attack

They cook the area around your tail bone. After a short period, depending on the intensity this may take 60 seconds or more, you will feel horrible cramps.

### Feeling

This pain makes you crawl on the floor.

Horrible torture

### After effects

It takes at least one hour before the horrible cramps get a little less painful.

How to detect normal cramps you will have other parts of your body react as well, like heavy sweating. In this case there is just intense pain.

## Diarrhea

They cook your intestines and you have a very strong feeling to go to the toilet. By continuously beaming you have very heavy diarrhea

**Why it is applied**

Keep you out of important events, e.g., A lawsuit where you have to defend yourself

## Erection termination

This beam makes your erection go away, if you are a man of course.

This can be done in 20-30 seconds. Depending on the direction of the beam your intestines may start bubbling though not very loud

## Urge to urinate

They beam your lower body so you will feel the urge to urinate.

It is difficult to ignore and there will come a moment you will have to do this when the beam continues.

**\*\*\*UPPER LEGS\*\*\***

## Block burst

The feeling is that your movement is blocked. You must take care not to fall or make a strange move

## ***KNEE***

### Short beams

This will cause pain to your knee

High intensity beaming

They put the beamer on your knee and make sure it stays there for hours. The location may vary but just above the knee cap can cause

a lot of pain. This will result in very much pain and a very sensitive knee.

### How it is applied

After a few days, your knee hurts a lot when walking. They may apply this also when biking to make you think something is wrong with your knee

### Feeling

Very painful, horrible torture

## ***LOWER LEGS***

### Calf cooking

They apply low intensity, low power beam to your legs, e.g., when you are in bed. Your muscles, legs feel stiff the next morning. They may start cooking the calf after you finished running, and after some time before you want to go running to prevent you from running

## How it is applied

What happens when you increase load on cooked muscles? They tear apart

## Feeling

Very painful, horrible torture

## Why it is applied

Prevent you from running, or other Sports

## Calf bursting

This beam is in fact a very high power burst and can cook your calf from hundreds of meters in a split second. If you are running your cooked muscles will tear apart and you have instant injury.

See: also, heart attack high power burst.

You may notice the following feeling: a needle going in and out of your calf within a second

## Feeling

Very painful, horrible torture

## Why it is applied

Prevent you from running or other sports

## Shin cooking

They cook the skin of your shin with very high intensities. When you are running, the shin injury is a well-known. They may start cooking the skin of your shin after you finished running, and after sometime (days) before you want to go running to prevent you from running

**Feeling**

Very painful, horrible torture

**Why it is applied**

Prevent you from running, other sports

## Heel muscle

The cook your heel muscle. This muscle does not contain much nerves so it is difficult to detect before the damage has been done. Then you will think back and remember there was something wrong the previous day or days.

**Feeling**

Walking can be painful.

**Why it is applied**

Prevent you from running, or other sports

## Ankle

They cook your ankles, just to cause you pain. You feel the beam and it is difficult to keep your leg in the same position because of the pain.

This is often applied for a long period of time, several hours.

**Feeling**

Very painful

**After effects**

May take several days to disappear when applied with high intensities

## Foot

They beam very hard in the center of your foot

**Feeling**

Very painful, horrible torture

## Foot insane

They burst the center of your foot with max power very short burst beam, only once while walking even in a crowded place. This causes insane pain and you may fall immediately, because the foot is not functioning anymore.

**Feeling**

Extremely painful, horrible torture

## Toes

They pick a single toe and beam it for several days in a row

**Feeling**

Painful

## Toes insane

They burst your toes with max power very short burst beam, and do this several times. This causes insane pain.

## How it is applied

They may do this while riding your bike, horrible torture

## Foot block

Ultrasonic beam to block the movement of a foot. If you are not prepared for this block you may fall.

### ***BODY***

## Shaking

Your whole body starts shaking like being in an aircraft in bed weather. The frequency is around 5 Hz. The intensity may amaze you.

## Scratching

They apply a scratch beam to any part of your body. This beam is very hard to resist. Before you know it, you may start scratching yourself like crazy

## Feeling

Horrible torture

## **LEG**

### Tremble apart

Some high-power acoustic beamer is aimed at your leg and after sometime your leg feels non-cooperative, not part of your body anymore

## ***MOOD***

### Sleepy feeling

They beam you with a frequency that makes you really feel sleepy. You will start yawning and cannot keep your eyes open. This effect starts very suddenly and often ends very abrupt.

### How it is applied

They may also do this by devices built into your car

### Nausea

Not a very pleasant feeling but not very disturbing or damaging

See the world turning     You feel dizzy and see the world turning like when you are very, very tired. This effect is not really very real. The moment you are out-of-the-beam you are not turning anymore. Still it is amazing that this can be done.

### Fatigue attacks

Forced awake

With this well-known beam, they will keep you awake, prevent you from sleeping. This way they wear you out, may be the next day you have an important meeting or must finish important work.

Sweating, nauseous, vomit feeling

You start sweating suddenly, you feel dizzy, you think you may have to vomit. When applied with enough intensity you will start to vomit, you will need at least 30 minutes to recover a little bit from this attack, but it will take hours before your body is acting a bit like before the attack.

## How it is applied

They may do this when you are with a friend. Google: Navy vomit beam

## Feeling

Horrible torture

### ***SLEEP***

## <u>Induce dreams</u>

You have strange dreams about things but the dreams are not like dreams you had before. The dreams may refer to very recent events in your life, like a person you met, a movie you saw, it is another form of reacting to events in your life.

## How it is applied

Some people in your environment might tell you they have wild dreams that night trying to get you talking about your experience

Links:

**Secret Service:** fear for the truth to be revealed! (17) Gang Stalkers and people cookers are murders, the crimes they commit belong to the worst crimes in history

Secret Service fear for the truth to be revealed (16) – A new category murderers: people cookers – cooking people like a microwave oven cooks meat

The Hidden Evil (by Mark Rich)

# MICROWAVE MIND CONTROL

### Tim Rifat

People cooker. com (in Dutch: mensenkoker.nl)

Secret Service: fear for the truth to be revealed! (15) – start independent investigations so they can be brought to justice and jailed

The normal people at war with the mentally ill (the Murderers and psychopaths)

Secret Service: fear for the truth to be revealed! (13) – normal people are murdered to keep the system running (the sick system needs blood to survive and expand)

Secret Service: fear for the truth to be revealed! (9) – use of electronic weapons (including mind invasive technology) to suggest psychiatric problems

Bio effects of Selected Non-Lethal Weapons

Electronic Torture

Electronische Wapens (in Dutch)

**To all politicians of the world:**

The only way to save the world is to stop your national secret services. Breaking laws and violating human rights in horrible ways has become a way of life. They are responsible for most problems in your neighborhood, in your city, in your country, in the world. Make them responsible for what they are doing. Let them account for in detail, force them to open up their organizations for thorough investigations. Stop their funding if they do not co-operate. Replace directors and staff immediately by normal people for starters.

Thanks to Peter Mooring and Deborah Dupre for this thorough information as references and the excellent graph and as whistleblowers. Please help to spread the message and/or donate:

STOPEG foundation – STOP Electronic weapons and Gang stalking: http://www.STOPEG.com

Stichting STOPEG – STOP Electronische wapens en Groepstalking:

http://www.STOP.NL (in Dutch)

Stichting STOPEG - STOP Electronische wapens en

Groepstalking: http://www.STOPEG.nl (in Dutch)

**Peter Mooring**

I again thank Peter for making this list available detailing his experiences with this technology as far away as the Netherlands.

What Peter is describing is identical to what I, and many others are experiencing globally and to the letter substantiating a global testing program.

**NOTE:** Regarding the Google image below, ask yourself is this an actual depiction of the factual full potential of what the microwave directed energy weapon can do when used as a tool for-extreme and horrific torture during war for example? If so, these weapons should be a matter of grave concern to humanity.

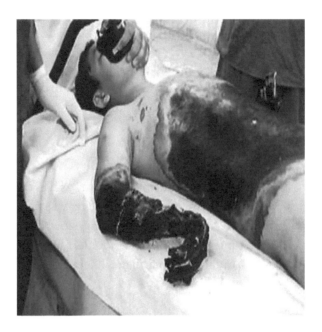

Perhaps the scariest thing of all is that even though this weapon has been indefinitely shelved - until such a time as we can agree on certain international laws pertaining to its ethical use in war, or so we are told, there are government, police, and tactical leaders who believe that a weaker version should be made and used to restrain violent protesters, and it is deadly when applied as relentless focused beam attacks on targets around the clock.

Here is an excellent video:

Microwave Weapon Use Today in America:

https://vimeo.com/187047877

As the painful torture, by continued focused of the energy weapon beam ravished my body around the clock, including my eyes and periodically my heart muscle to frighten me into submission, a sinister pattern began to emerge by those angered that they had not controlled or neutralized me.

They continued to request, "Stop those books and we will leave you alone." This was to ensure that I knew why they were doing this to me, or so they said, reinforced by the escalating severity of the attacks. The message, "If I did not, you are dead."

I could and would not.

At times, we have to stand no matter what. What these "Covert Technological Monsters" were intentionally doing was now redirecting the beam with renewed accuracy and ongoing slow deterioration of now my all of my joints, cooking my shoulders, ankles, wrists, leg bones, the bottom of my feet, ear cartilage, knees, etc., etc., etc.

After the successful deterioration of already two hips joints advanced to a condition out of the ordinary and medically impossible, still believing it could not be proven, or that typically no one believes targets, the beam terrorizing continued. I covered my knees at home with protective material all day. When I did the beam then refocused on both shoulder joints as I worked at my computer. While sleeping the beam focused on my hands, wrist and ankle joints. While successfully protected in the bunker I devised, and slept inside each night, around my bed, if my foot became exposed while sleeping, by tossing and turning, they targeted foot waking me by burning searing pain.

My whole body began to crack when I moved from depletion of synovial fluids vital to joint normal for healthy functioning and movement. The only thing that made them back off was exposure which I did around the clock on several social networks of which they monitored.

Ultimately, the end result of the relentless attacks to my joints, by the focused Directed Energy Weapon beam, could and would become Autoimmune Joint Disease.

Degenerative joint diseases such as osteoarthritis and autoimmune diseases affecting the joints are painful and debilitating and they were escalating this condition synthetically and technologically in my body.

While some joint diseases are considered to be the "normal" wear and tear of joints and bones due to aging, other joint diseases are due to the body's immune system attacking healthy joint tissue for a variety of reasons. In my case, my body's immune system was not attacking healthy joint tissue, those viciously targeting me from a state-of-the-art military /law enforcement counter-terrorism division were and alternating with their advanced weapon equipped drones. When I left home at night to pick-up take-out a drone followed me East, West, North and South. When I returned home, it returned to its position over my home and woke me in the wee hours of the morning in pain or the nervous system vibrating hum mm, hum mm, hum mm of the Sonic Weapon.

One night when I went outside and used my camera phone taking pictures of them, the hum mm immediately stopped and the lights went off in one of the locations there were using.

They were determined that they would ultimately win by maliciously destroying my health coupled with the certainty, repeated over and over and over again, that it could not be proven and would be determined, to have originated from some other source and that I would instead be deemed crazy. This was likely the assessment after careful review, of my medical history looking for any weakness to exploit such as my right ankle severely damaged in 2007, in a major car accident directly related to my first not knowing what was evolving around me or that this is beyond a doubt an ongoing human experimentation of which no one is exempt.

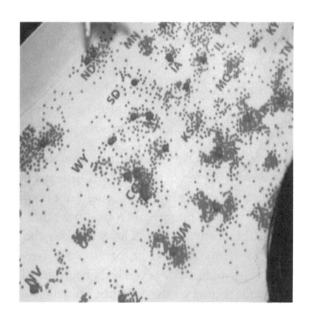

Map showing clusters of Targeted Individuals within the U.S. as seen on TruTV, Conspiracy Theory with Jesse Ventura episode entitled "Brain Invaders" December 2012

# CHAPTER FIVE
# Till Death Do We Part

By July of 2013, I had to face the reality that I had been marked for death and that my efforts and growing audience was in fact a life saver, by a fused effort between the military and law enforcement, and modern COINTELPRO. I simply was expendable if it meant unwanted exposure of program machinations that I and many others are fighting for our lives for weapon exposure. It still appeared to be mainly a group of African American men strategically placed around me spearheading the attacks, however, without any real power in America, they were there because of their leadership in a leased location their worksite. "THEY want her" was also another series of repetitive threats as the foundation for extreme attacks.

It really hits home after I realized that the only outcome from the night after night, day after day physical attacks was ultimately eventual slow death, through systematic breaking down of one body part after another creating a domino effect and that the leadership had given approval for the long haul. The body can only take so much. And their continuing to up the ante the after watching my various projects, accelerated the torture, which was also based on my refusal to stop. Another favored, repetitive threat was and is to this day, "She thinks we are playing with her." The desire to prove they were not, seemed to motivate them to higher and higher depths of severe, barbaric life-threatening torture on occasions.

This specific group, in my opinion, brings uniqueness to my targeting and their leadership strategically knew it. I believe the uniqueness results from environments with some having a silly gangster mentality with little real opportunities, originating from a disenfranchised community. This is a clue to how some of them perceive themselves and the length they were willing to go to and is also the key to understanding the resulting behavior and how both could be deadly. Who is deadlier than the leadership actually pulling the strings and giving official approval? What they were doing could not happen any other way.

It later dawned on me that these men and their leadership appeared extremely eager to prove themselves to their supervisors at various levels and this fact alone guaranteed that they would take my life at the drop of a dime and even quicker if given the go ahead or the livelihood of both puppet and pawn in jeopardy.

And, with the threat of possible job loss they appeared more than willing to prove their worth, push the torture to the hilt and to levels, of which could easily result in attempted murder.

Let's be franks, in reality, black men have zero power in America. Some would argue that they were being used to hurt me, but in my opinion, appear in total agreement with their supervisors' due to thwarted egotism with both, as a result of their inability to impact me the way they intended, a proven success, and who were now passing the buck. In fact, in mid-August, one of the African American men actually said, "They" want us to murder her" intentionally for me to hear him as I began pulling this book together for final publication. Trust me; I do not for one minute believe that these men are on my side one bit. Their loyalty lies with those who sign their paychecks.

When they began repeatedly accusing me of believing they were playing with me, or that I had made them look bad, I could not help but wonder, if they now wanted to do a drive-by after everything else failed? The leadership was more into randomly created attacks with casualties.

Let me correct this last statement regarding their failure. They had in fact been totally successful and effective in crippling me, however, I was not going to let it stop my fight for justice and exposure and cower. And, after the February 2017, assisted fall down the stairs, breaking the deteriorated other hip. I slid on my belly for an hour to get to my car in my garage then drove 60 miles to the VA hospital only to learn the severity. I actually made it to the parking of the West Los Angeles VA hospital before the Fire Department had to be called to lift me from my vehicle and take me inside. That morning I have been turned away from the local hospital in my community after I witnessed a local sheriff and USAF person showing up and it then insinuated and being accused of nothing being wrong with me.

Ego driven, this operation appeared to be murderously, extremely offended by my lack of recognition of their importance and some even appeared almost insulted by my shunning their complements. They likely had great success with some.

This is the personality of which many, many targets will validate predominant in these groups hired to do this type of work in general.

Let me state for the record, that I owe no allegiance to any group or race, attempting to take my life, degrade me, and systematically destroy my body. Nor do I consider you friends and we friendly. There is good and bad in everyone, and I consider myself part of the human race. However, the black men were likely assigned to deflect the malicious treatment in this program being directed at me which could appear racially motivated if done by another race although others were surely involved also and people of all races are suffering equally.

Perhaps what brought this realization home regarding the race card was one of them who said, "THEY" are the ones making us do this to you." The key word here is someone else is making them hurt me so severely. And without a doubt, the young white military personnel were just a vicious on assignment by use of these weapons, as well as contractors, and the officiated trained recruits of all races. blaming as it is someone else's fault.

When this stated was followed by "This is how we earn our living," I was totally disgusted with them as a whole recognizing this as the real truth.

In other words, I was being told that they had to slowly murder to me because, if they did not, they would lose their jobs. from

Sadly, many times, both white and black, they are unqualified, to do anything else and in desperation too keep employment they believed brought them some sort of prestige would become deadly for me.

These group, masked inherent self-hatred, and hatred of others combined with a verbalized belief that I had made them look bad. This is while rightfully fighting for my life, truth the weapon.

Just prior to going to the gym each day, after deciphering my thoughts and plans for the day, they cooked my legs so severely that once, after making it to the gym, I was in so much pain that I could not get out of the car and turned around and went back home. The objective is to affect the quality of a target's life and even appearance. Another objective is to send a message of their power through this technology that even if they cannot control your mind fully, they certainly can through the creation of crippling pain control to your body proven highly effective.

For example, while at the doctor's office one day, the doctor said, "I see you have back pain." I immediately said no. I had completely forgotten that in 2006, seven years ago, I was seen at the hospital for back pain for a brief period. After the doctor made this declaration during this appointment in 2013, again watched in real-time, the next morning I woke in such intense back pain that I literally could hardly get out of bed.

Miraculously the pain erupted right after the doctor mentioned it the day before. A few days later, my 26-year-old, middle daughter, phoned from Denver, after having had to be taken to the hospital with back pain so powerful that she fell down, and was not able to get back up, through mysterious back pain materializing out of nowhere as the threats continued to harm my children and make sure I knew it. Was this yet another message to frighten me and to prove, "We can and will get to your daughters too?" If it were not a message, they surely had told me repeatedly, during their eight-year crucifixion and involvement in my life this saying that they could and surely would do so if I did not comply, meaning harm my children.

While visiting Denver, in April of 2013, one month after the birth of my new granddaughter, I could not only hear, but feel the global weapon system searing the muscles of my legs rendering me barely able to walk during my entire visit. This was used to embarrass me as I limped around like a cripple among people I had not seen in years. I had been given a brief reprieve from the torture about five days before I left which returned my gait to some degree of normalcy and the pain had begun to subside. I became happy and hopeful. But this was later obvious PsyOps when the pain beam hit with a vengeance upon arrival. With family, the game plan is to prove that we can and will get to you, and your family, no matter where you are on the face of the Earth and we control your body.

Some people over time have suggested that I need to be nicer to them, understanding their power-driven mentality, for example the representative in my Congressman's office and believed this might result in their letting up on torturing me. However, one thing I understood completely, ALL of these men are predators across the board and apparently by nature. That includes those pulling to the strings, to those actually pushing the buttons.

I would never submit to this group under any circumstances or for any reason and again, they are just going to happen to kill me or come into the open. The later, under the circumstances and as time progressed and exposure begin to snowball was not an option without full disclosure of how the technology is being used today. This is the last thing they want brought before any Court system.

I am just passing through here and whatever good I can do, I am determined to do it.

They were rightfully concerned with exposure of this program and what exposure could do to their operation and any participating organization or agency involved because of unethical tactics. This had become the foundation for them literally, Hell bent on destroying my life and telling me also that of my daughters who were just starting out in the world. These books appear to have become a deadly Achilles Heel.

After repeating over and over again, "She's smart," because of my determination to write these books and see them to fruition through great pain and sacrifice, hard to break victims, become a challenge to all of them because of this perception and as stated early the conceited perceptions of themselves. However, whereas it appeared that the black men were trying to prove their worth or that they were "smart too" through extreme abuse, the whites involved appeared to believe themselves superior naturally and me inferior.

In fact, as I sat at my laptop computer to begin writing this book I realized that in fact my life depended on it 100. I had no choice but to continue or until Till Death Do We Part. I had already been told that they were never leaving after now eight years ago. I would keep writing and perhaps I would also get that book of targeted individual short stories I had initially hoped, which would provide the much-needed additional targeted individual credibility necessary for all victims as confirmation.

I could hear the weekend shift making the typical comments familiar to many in this program by use of the technology called Hypersonic Sound Device letting me know they were ever present and watching my every move and listening to my every sub-vocal thought.

What is interesting about the sub-vocal thought reading capability is that the technology appears to pick up on thoughts before the target registers it as a valid thought or it is verbalized in your mind. For example, I got up to go upstairs, and without thinking about it or verbalizing the thought inside my head, checked the door to make sure it was locked. I immediately heard one say, "She's scared." I was not.

It was an instinct that they were reading based on the limited perceptions of the five senses which constantly report wrong information.

To me this is one of the great injustices and handicaps of this technology in the hands of morons. In reality, they are interpreting information passing through the mind of a target, sub-vocally, and then depicting it as accurate which makes this technology morally wrong. A random thought is then used to harass the target with things they may have felt but did not think verbally but sub-vocally, as being a true thought and the target's belief.

I worked for about two hours after waking one morning then got up to go downstairs for breakfast. As I did, I typically heard the beam in the ceiling moving along with me. This I knew is a sure sign of drone satellite viewing by the all too familiar creaking noise it makes when positioning itself inside the ceiling ready to follow me downstairs. I then immediately felt the beam attacking my upper hip area. "What is the point?" I thought to myself, as I stood, and cringed in pain from the right hip pain then slid down the stairs.

In late April and early May of 2013, I was taken from my home twice by ambulance. The first time was after severe attacks to my knees during the night left me barely able to make it down the stairs of my home as my knees buckled and I was at risk of falling and killing myself which could appear as accidental. The second time was due to the directed energy weapon focusing on the left side of my neck for days then moving to the top of my left shoulder for an extended period, then gradually making its way to over to my heart muscle again and again.

The average person does not know that Russia claims to have a psychotronic computer virus called "Satan 666".

The system purportedly can cause heart attacks. Putin said in Forbes that psychotronic weapons that attack the body with electromagnetic energy are as powerful as the atom bomb

Emergency room doctors at my local hospital would also document the uncharacteristic nature of the beginning stages of knee deterioration, which usually shows calcification in the knees of which I had none yet early deterioration was still present. Another ER doctor would document, that the unexplained symptoms I explained as materialization of pain in my neck, left shoulder, left arm, and hand, and the numbness in my hand that the symptoms appeared to originate from an unknown etiology after tests revealed a completely normal electrocardiogram of my heart and the excessive heart rate these operations create, in the emergency room.

Military and intelligence agencies have developed frightful electronic weapons in black budget projects over the last decades capable of efficient murder. These weapons are called non-lethal or less than lethal because they are designed to be applied only for a very short period with the intention of briefly incapacitating a person or designed to make people get out of the beam's ray when used for riot or crowd control dispersal. They are designed to not kill a person immediately when used in this manner.

However, these weapons today are being used in extreme ways today. These weapons are in fact the perfect Weapons of Mass Destruction, and the perfect crime.

A psychopath or sociopath is a personality trait or disorder characterized partly by enduring antisocial behavior, a diminished capacity for empathy or remorse, and poor behavioral controls. Anti-social behavior is behavior that lacks consideration for others that can cause damage to the society, whether intentionally or through negligence.

So many human lives are being destroyed in this definite technology testing program. And I can't say enough that these efforts thrive because many cannot comprehend, imagine, or more importantly believe that such evil efforts exist or that trusted authority figures, whom we are taught or programmed to respect from childhood and honor are capable of these atrocities today.

Poor behavior controls in these groups is obvious in the see saw method of their PsyOps.

Human behavior refers to a range of behaviors exhibited by humans of which are influenced by culture, attitudes, emotions, values, ethics, again, authority, rapport, hypnosis, persuasion, coercion and/or genetics. The behavior of people, and other organisms or even mechanisms, falls within a range with some behavior being common, some unusual, some acceptable, and some outside acceptable limits.

These programs continue to flourish and has flourished secretively for decades within the Military Industrial Complex and other highly places government agencies, many Department of Defense contractors without a doubt. Today many are experiencing the effects of these nothing less than brilliant systems and devices, which left a trail of human lab rats, and the resulting official patents, being used not for the good of humanity good but for evil, inflicting pain and destruction.

Many psychopaths are able to appear as an "average everyday persons."

I imagine that people who get addicted to killing others legally in this program, would have to have no empathy or remorse for their actions, deeply programmed and therefore they are more than likely psychopathic, sociopathic, or suffering from anti-social personality disorder. There's but a small difference between the illnesses.

The thrill a person gets from watching horror movies is an adrenaline rush many will agree. Anyone that murders someone and gets away with it, can become addicted to the thrill and a specific type of adrenaline rush and this type of physical rush can be addicting as can also the thrill and adrenalin rush of torturing someone obviously. Many deranged individuals start out torturing animals for the thrill.

The adrenaline rushes can cause an adrenaline high, and again, can become addicting due to a chemical released in the body. Then add to this scenario the ability to do heinous things without getting caught, or by official approval it may convince the person to continue to hurt another or worse for personal gain or satisfaction in some way guilt free.

Some factually kill for the power surge they get from committing this act and the elation of again feeling like God through holding another person's life in their hands. A psychopath uses to be defined as a "moral imbecile" or someone without conscience, free of all moral constraints. Psychologists are still arguing whether psychopaths are created by nature or nurtured from childhood abuse, mental incapacity, or more important of all, the criminal culture of today. However, there is little to no awareness of mind invasive technology that mimics mental illness and effectively create the exact same symptoms.

Those working in these programs believe themselves dominant, over others through the technology, and when combined with grossly distorted egotism or a "Do you know who I am and what I can do to you" mentalities are extremely dangerous and definitely psychopathic.

Regarding the God complex for example, Donald Henry Gaskins, was dubbed the redneck Charles Manson, in the book Final Truth written by Wilton Earl. Gaskins was reported as declaring: "I have walked the same path as God; by taking lives and making others afraid, I became God's equal.

This powerful statement is a hint at the motivation and urges that could drive even an average man to murder another in these program by legalization that penetrates to conscious and sub consciousness.

The greatest thrill of all for those capable of murder is the power of playing God which would lay dormant until ignited, say for example, again, in a legalized government secretive technology testing program of which the individuals feel to their advantage could not be traced, leaves no evidence, and whereas they could enjoy the thrill of playing God without exposure. Add to use of technology intentionally designed to give the appearance of playing a video game on a computer as well as the physical detachment of not being in the same room or up close to the victim with a gun or knife and presto.

This technology does so many things. It can talk to you inside you head, read your mind, create death and illness, and so much more.

As I have said before, these are characteristics once thought only within the power of a Supreme Being or Creator.

These people given the right circumstances and opportunity may have the potential to be thrill killers by "Covert Technological Murder resulting from non-face to face contact and the disassociation.

Ask any Targeted Individual if "That's Impossible" meaning to be attacked by directed energy weapons, inside and outside of their homes, around the clock for days, months and even years, and they will tell you, unequivocally, absolutely not and from there painful and personal experiences.

Murderers see themselves as dominant, controlling and powerful figures. They perceive themselves as holding the power of life and death in their hands.

Perhaps those working in these programs were once moral ethical men before being intoxicated by the power of torturing a person literally to death and not just one but many people.

Today, by appearance, they appear to have become so corrupted and the smell of ultimate death resulting in successful operations and enjoyment of pain and suffering that they can no longer be characterized as honorable men and have lost the ability of moral separation from what is truly just plain wrong with no justification.

It is Sunday morning in 2018 and typical of the shift that comes in from 10:30 p.m. till around 6:30 a.m.; their job is to try implanting thoughts into my head or anyone around me while sleeping to benefit the effort. Many a morning they watch me like a hawk waiting for me to wake and then believing I have been sufficiently programmed by subliminal comments while I slept during the night are disappointed when I wake and it has not worked for the umpteen time. What happens next is they become angry then turn up the microwave weapon torture.

My oldest daughter was visiting one weekend, and as soon as I woke, "Get her daughter" was verbalized as I opened my eyes.

Other mornings as they watched me get out of bed, "She does not care. She went straight to the computer and that book she is now writing" which then ignites their wrath and torture.

One morning there was an argument with my daughter, prompted 100% by them. During my 30-year-old daughter's visit, they had her so scared after using the hologram technology to broadcast an image of a ghoul one night a few years ago around her waking her in the wee hours of the morning. I woke fussing because she has been sleeping with the light on in her bedroom and locking the door. I am fussing not because this is the behavior of a 5-year-old still afraid of the Boogey Man but because I know the objective of those around me and anyone around me is to create fear and control. It is just unacceptable.

She then tells me that she is really frightened of me, that I might kill her. LOL! And this is the reason, she felt the need to lock the door and sleep with the light on. She said that this was after me telling her of Jeremiah's story and how mind control technology was used in an attempt to nudge him into attempted murder of his parents. I tell her she missed the whole point; the point is that Jeremiah did not do that which they tried very hard to force him into doing.

Although I was upset that she thought me capable of this, I still understood. It was likely beamed to her while she slept, I was also sure.

Jeremiah's story is an example of the extreme power of electromagnetic manipulation and sadly there are similar success stories of victims resulting in loss of life each day making the news.

However, I remind her that most, being manipulated are unaware of what is happening through lack knowledge of the capabilities of the technology in use, and the obvious fact that they have consistently, repeatedly, failed with thousands.

Again, Hell will freeze over before I allow people I have concluded are complete and utterly ridiculous fools control me. These books of which they desperately want stopped is an example of them not controlling my life, I tell her. They just do not want book publication, are going to extremes, to include using her, to stop me and others, and I tell her that if they had control over me, they would not be in existence.

As I drove my daughter home, after dropping her off, I had the urge to immediately urinate which was so powerful that I had to exit the freeway. After I got back onto the freeway, I immediately had to go again, and had to exit the freeway again.

When I arrived back home, I see the neighbor outside watering his grass from the location that I have been feeling the portable beam lately. I have two books inside my car and turn around, speak briefly with him about my plight, give him copies of the two other books and tell him, of this new book, as Book II in my series, to be released by late fall of 2013. Later while at home and upstairs documenting this morning's activities, I hear the neighbor on my right side, calling me a "Fucking H" then drive off from the house which had the mystery guests living there for months. I wonder if he even knows what prompted him to say this or that it could be beamed into empty heads. They are undoubtedly pissed that their effort to convince me that I am something that I am not nor has ever been has failed and that the efforts appears to be back firing in their faces, as they continue to put on a façade for the rest of the world.

After working all day, I decide to call it a night around 11:00 p.m.

Because I still have energy, I decide to go out the gym instead. As I pulled out of my garage, I immediately notice the bright light on in the elderly man next door's bedroom parallel to my bedroom and where I had been working. Experience has taught me that someone is there and has set up the portable microwave pain beam and had been waiting for me to go to bed to turn it on me. They are just going to have to wait until I come back home of which they surely will.

On another night, I again am working until late, this time around 1:00 a.m. I decide to call it a night not wanting to exhaust myself for the next day. I turn off my laptop and prepare for bed. Once in bed, I feel the intensity of the portable microwave Directed Energy Weapon irradiating my body from the elderly neighbor's spare bedroom again adjacent to my bedroom which is about 20 feet away and also upstairs.

I get up and position the protective material against the wall then get back into bed. I then feel my body humming from the toxic radiation and it is now coming from the floor beneath my bed upwards. I have a thick rubber mat used for gym floors in the closet which I purchased it new as a 5 x 5 piece after learning it is effective for deflection. I get out of bed, retrieve it, place it under me, and then was able to fall asleep.

Make no mistake about the military's major role, in some of the most heinous activities in these testing programs overall. This technology originated with the military before trickling down to law enforcement. GIs also known as Government Issues are in the business of war and indoctrinated into this mentality as service members in Basic Training of which I know all too well.

When I considered a Federal Tort Claim against the United States Air Force base, obviously involved, and about 40 miles from my current residence, which has the large microwave tower pointing in the direction of my home, I phone the legal office of the Judge Advocate General (JAG) on the base several times and the line kept being mysteriously disconnected by those monitoring my phone calls.

Hmm mm. I also have the misfortune, I later learned, of inadvertently moving, without advance knowledge, to an area about 10 minutes away from one of Lockheed Martin's major sites which is naturally positioned close to the Air Force base and a major contractor who specialize in the microwave Directed Energy Weapon System. I realize that I have gone from the frying pan, now into the fire, now surrounded with primary agencies involved in what is happening today to include police neighbors, and military reserve personnel as well who are reserve. Reserve personnel are also those assigned as operatives in this program.

An example of the mind reading software in prevalent use today is the MALINTENT. It is a system that went into field operation testing in 2008 which is marketed as turning the logical approach of threat reduction on its head by profiling everyone.

Homeland Security had an operational field test in Maryland, scanning 144 unwitting human subjects. Results are confidential, testing is ongoing and further disclosure could compromise continued testing the department reports. In other words, they want to keep the truth of mind invasive technology in secrecy.

Here are two authentic examples, above and below the next page of MALINTENT computerized Electro-encephalograph (EEG) thought deciphering and mind reading computerized software accomplished effortlessly by reading brainwave patterns effortlessly by an operator from his workstation during a presentation.

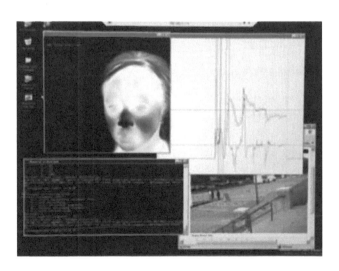

# CHAPTER SIX
# Gaslighting

The objective of the games continues to be discrediting the target as a nutcase by any means necessary. Make no mistake about this fact; it is first and far most one of the primary goals equal only to creating fear, influencing, and torture.

Because of this, moving furniture around inside a target's home can play a pivotal role in getting a target to second guess and question his or her mental stability on a personal level. "Did I put that there?" "Did I move that?" This tactic is then combined with the use of drones which make sounds inside of a targets home sounding as if, whomever entered the home and moved things around earlier is coming in again while you are alone at night. This is while the operation center deciphers your thoughts hoping for the fear factor at every turn.

When I first heard of a covert discrediting tactic called Gas lighting, it was from an old friend in 2004. During a general conversation while out at dinner one night, he began telling me about a relationship in which he had just gotten out of claiming the woman he was dating, a high-ranking female at the Sheriff's Department in Los Angeles was a nutcase. He began to detail to me the issues she was having at work after someone decided that she was no longer desirable due to personality conflicts. I remember my friend, a psychiatric nurse telling me that he stopped dating the woman because she kept telling him that things were being moved around inside her house unexplainably.

This included furniture being moved from one location to another after she had placed it in a certain permanent location, to include her hair dryer out of its typical place, a creature of habit, in her bathroom and sitting on her kitchen counter when she came home one day and the list went on.

I would later realize how grateful I was that he had talked with me about this when it began happening to me. As a result of this forewarning, when I came home and the following things had been moved, I was not alarmed and coincidentally, I now lived in an area where the Los Angeles County Sheriff's department has jurisdiction. One thing I knew for certain, nothing happened without their knowing about it to include a full-scale targeting operation.

1. The trash can in one of my bathrooms upstairs was moved and was now sitting in the middle of the bathroom floor out of its normal position.

2. A USB which had my Federal Tort Claim legal action information saved on it went missing.

    When this happened, I immediately called my landlords to complain, believing that they had given someone the key to get in. However, it is a document fact that covert entry classes are offered to law enforcement in California and nationwide. In this type of targeting operations, they know nothing is happening inside your home. This part of highly effective PsyWar tactics typically materializing after death threats saying, we can get to you whenever we want too. In reality if they want to kill you, a zapped heart attack while alone at home is highly effective in the cover-up or perhaps a beamed brain aneurysm.

    I would later learn that key bumping a door for entry can be accomplished in less than 15 seconds. This is way victims should invest in heavy duty security locks, which are costly but worth it.

    During the targeting, law enforcement had entered my home two other times, in Anaheim California in 2006, and also in Arizona in 2009. Each of these times they intentionally left visible signs of entry as a form of hopeful intimidation and even in Anaheim left entrapping bait.

However, when the USB went missing in early 2013, I had had three sitting next to each other and miraculously they had taken the wrong one.

After witnessing my called to the landlord, and lack of fear, the other disk miraculously reappeared downstairs on the kitchen counter when I came home another day. I can guarantee it was not there after I cleaning the kitchen before I left.

3.  I came home and the sink stopper had been completely taken out of my downstairs guest bathroom and placed on top of the sink counter. It is impossible for it to jump out of the sink on its own.

4.  The remote control for the television in my family room was now upstairs sitting on my bed, right next to the remote for the bedroom television sitting side by side neatly lined up next to each other by obvious intent.

5.  After spending a Sunday cleaning, dusting, polishing and shining everything, a day later, when I returned home from the gym, my glass dinner table had fingerprint, and handprint smudge marks on it and the chair was pushed back from the table as if someone had sat down and did not put it back when they stood to leave.

6.  One of the first things I notice but did not pay much attention to prior to these series of events, at first was the coffee table was moved which sits in front of my sofa and was now sitting at an angle to my couch instead of aligned.

Of these incidences, it was the remote being moved, from downstairs to upstairs, that was an eye opener. Although I have had previous experience with the radar laser beam being able to manipulate electrical instruments, such as house smoke detectors, or even rattle a gate when I walked by late one night in Arizona as a test for fear, or even hold your arms and hands down to prevent my typing on my computer by a powerful beamed force, it appeared that this operation when I dwelled on the remote being neatly sitting next to each other, thought they finally had my attention. They had not. I took the other remote back downstairs where it belonged, then turned on my TV upstairs and began watching a movie and forgot about it which is not what they wanted.

Believe it or not, moving limbs of your body or restricting them is also similar to a report by Jeremiah Ivie.

Jeremiah Ivie stated, during his You Tube, interview that the technology was used one day to force him to lift his hand to his nose, and his finger touch his nose against his will. However, regarding the remote being move from downstairs to upstairs, I did not think that the technology could levitate the remote and float it from downstairs in my family room to upstairs in my bedroom? It had to be moved.

My hands had been held down with my being unable to move them to my astonishment one day as well. After a night of sexual stimulation those in the operation center watched me prepare to write yet another letter complaining about this dirty, unwanted behavior to about ten officials in Washington D.C., after getting their email address on line. I literally could not lift my hands to my laptop to type the letter and it felt like a ton of invisible bricks were on top of my hands holding my arms and hands down. I was amazed then angered.

From past experience, in nearly every location I had live, everyone, within the community knew I was a target to include landlords but again, I doubt if they knew the outcome or high-tech advancement of the technology being used. I immediately called the landlord to complain after the remote incident and threatened that if it happened again, I would stop paying the rent, put their money into a separate bank account and let the eviction process began as an effort to bring any type of judicial intervention and awareness to any type of judge, regarding the illegally entering my home. The entrance was all about the specific agenda to create the perception of victims as crazy.

Believing that this threat would stop someone from toying with me, I felt assured that it would not happen again, until I came in and the decorate pillows on my loveseat were rearranged in a manner that was odd and my attention was immediately drawn to the new arrangement as soon as I entered my residence from the garage.

The bottom line is that with the covert technological harassment, attempts and community Gang / Organized stalking effort, I was 100% being officially Gas lighted. One night with the curtains still open to my large backyard, I could almost feel the presence of a male outside just standing there hoping to scare me. He later reminded me of a sheriff who would come to the gym and sit around me in the pool area a few times who did not know that I heard him tell someone what he did for a living and who later tried to pretend that he did something else instead when I asked him.

With the landlords, I had to make sure to inform them that I was not so nice in this battle for my life. I did this as a forewarning to action I would take to protect my life and the privacy of my residence if necessary.

As mentioned, the effort around me has always been to create dissention in my environment using any one around me they possibly could electromagnetically. Several times, I observed an odd expression on my female landlord's face as I spoke with her husband and she was out of the room and returned. To my amusement it appeared that she felt that I was interested in her elderly Jewish husband which most certainly, unequivocally had to be a suggestion planted in her head from the operation center while around me. Once when he was realigning my bathroom shower door in the master bathroom, she left to go down to their vehicle to get a tool for him. When she returned, I was in the bathroom with him, standing a short distance away, watching to see how he managed to get the shower door back on track after I had tried and failed several times. When she came back up the stairs she looked like a deer caught in headlights as she watched me standing there watching him in my bathroom. It was totally illogical.

The games these people are enjoying playing are not funny to the unaware. This is especially true when they are using technology which is taking over human thought and implanting things that the person normally would not consider or think of or playing on a person's insecurities, low self-esteem, or intentionally creating negativity by high-tech mental invasion.

A brief excerpt of the Gas Lighting definition from Wikipedia, the free encyclopedia is:

Gas lighting is forms of psychological abuse in which false information is presented with the intent of making a victim doubt his or her own memory, perception and sanity. Instances may range simply from the denial by an abuser that previous abusive incidents ever occurred, up to the staging of bizarre events by the abuser with the intention of disorienting the victim.

The term "gas lighting" comes from the play Gas Light and its film adaptations. The term is now also used in clinical and research literature.

Doing this to me was complete and utter nonsense. When I posted what was happening on Facebook, many people responded detailing what was happening to them in this same manner and all confirming was the result of modern COINTELPRO stalking. And many of the response postings from Facebook friends later detailing these incidents and mines miraculously disappeared due to all aspect of my life being hacked. I guess they did not want it known that they will enter your residence and want instead to create their own reality for the victim.

Below is a factual class schedule which offers training in lock picking classes and covert entry which are routinely offered to law enforcement, as exampled below and the training includes those involved in joint or fused (Fusion) efforts employed in Fusion centers as evidenced by the training schedule for the summer of 2013:

July 27, 2013 – Saturday

Covert Lock Picking, Bypass, Tactics and Techniques

Commerce, CA

August 05-06, 2013; Monday – Tuesday

Covert Entry Specialist I

Upland, CA - Upland Police Department

August 07-09, 2013; Wednesday – Friday

Covert Entry Specialist II Course

Upland, CA - Upland Police Department

September 28, 2013 – Saturday

Covert Lock Picking, Bypass, Tactics and Techniques

Another vital class listed on this training schedule:

September 25, 2013 – Wednesday

War Room Orientation

Law Enforcement Only!

The war is typically the nucleus and location of highly advanced technology and deployment of what is termed "Black Bag" technology.

The powerful beam attacks coming from the top of my ceiling downward was definitely the result of an aerial drone.

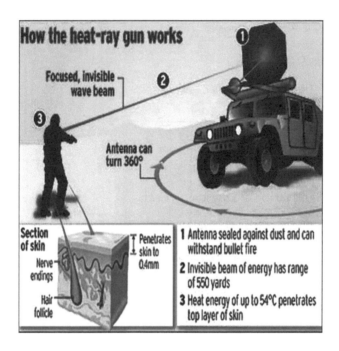

Easy technology tracking and directed energy weapon targeting, inside and outside of your home, and while travelling.

# CHAPTER SEVEN
# The Injustice System

In February of 2013, I was able to capture one of the men around me calling me a "B," while listening to a voicemail recording sent to my cellular phone. Those who monitored my phone were a different agency than the ones operating in the operation center it seemed at times. I also learned that they also at times appear to change their voice to sound ethnic instead of white.

This time the voice appeared to be one of the non-African American men sounding extremely angry at my taping the voicemail message from a hospital doctor for hopeful court proceedings. The doctor was trying to cover herself after she realized that I was not crazy and was beginning court proceedings naively, after she had told me of quite possibly, this same male captured on tape, contacted her and trying to have me involuntarily committed to the psyche ward which I document in "You Are Not My Big Brother."

As long as she thought my allegations were delusions, I was amusing to her as she played with me like a small child.

Essentially the voicemail detailed her attempt to cover herself, after revealing to me what had transpired when this official repeatedly tried to reach her, on her off-duty day at home. This was after I had gone in alone to speak with him about what and why was happening around me or if any connection as was being insinuated which I did not understand. He was amused during the meeting until I told him about the first book.

With the recorded phone message, I thought I finally had something for hopeful legal action and my effort to bring my plight into the justice system and eventual relief from the horrific coercive torture at the very least. I had tried and failed once before ridiculously filing Pro Se.

Perhaps I could get relief and justice by filing a Federal Tort Claim due to the extreme emotional abuse, psychological, and physical debilitating damage to my body by the energy weapon, and the apparent group decisive efforts continuing to this day to push me over the edge I now hoped.

I was then and now left with no other choice, as I had been the first time, but to seek hopeful judicial intervention yet again as my only recourse. Who do you go to when it is those you trust to do what is right doing this to you?

Typical of every target bringing these issues into the justice system, many of us are literally laughed out of court, and many of us have been deemed delusional regarding allegations listed as a fictitious government conspiracy in court records or similarly worded. This has occurred across the board when many of us have gone after specifically the government the Defendant in these cases.

James Walbert, if you remember, from Book One received some short-term relief through a restraining order granting. This was only as a result of going after, initially, a private citizen.

They just were not going to stop torturing me due to being able to do so while essentially in hiding in their center miles away along, or compliant neighboring locations, with the characteristic of it being done literally invisibly.

To my dismay, I also had no other choice, once again, but to again try to also represent myself without an attorney using the Pro Se Clinic believe with their help I had a shot.

Because of the magnitude of a case like this, many did not want to get involved along with the difficulty of proving the case and of course my lack of finances, also a major issue. I did not have money for the pricey legal fees to even start.

For this reason, I felt that a Federal Tort Claim would be less complicated for me due to it being one on one before a federal judge. However, the process of initiating court proceedings using any format can be daunting. This is especially true for someone with absolutely no legal experience and, again, no attorney eager to step into the cesspool focused around the lives of targets. The expertise and educated efforts would be required the ability to pull back layers of intentional secrecy of any specific agency or agencies involvement, and then challenge the power of Big Brother backing the agency and "The Program" and more importantly, this time around the legalization of DOD Regulations, US Codes, Executive Orders, Patriot Act, etc.

I wanted an attorney, but no one wanted to get involved in what still consistently appears to be a hopeless situation of which many targeted individuals find themselves at loss and have learned after fruitlessness usually results in continued and at times escalated suffering. Now more than ever the phrase, "Any person who represents themselves in court proceedings as his/her own attorney, has a fool for a client," rang with a powerful note of accuracy.

I remembered that I had the response to the Federal Tort Claim Administrative Action I filed in March of 2013 response letter in the glove compartment of my car. It was dated June 24, 2013. It was now August. I read through it again to see exactly how long I had to file a case against the United States instead of a specific agency. It read that I had 6 months. I hoped to begin the process before the time period lapsed.

The response letter had what I felt was a glimmer of hope with the author, a government attorney pointing out that the situation of which I detailed in the Federal Tort legal papers I sent appeared to be more consistent with criminal behavior around me saying:

To the extent that your allegation implicates possible instances of criminal conduct, such matters are outside Office of the General

Counsel to investigate. The Office of the Inspector General (IG) investigates criminal matters. If the IG substantiates the allegations of a claim, they can report the matter to the United States Attorney's Office for possible criminal prosecution…

This paragraph, however, appeared to also mock victims.

The U.S. Attorney's office is the office responsible for approving Electronic Surveillance efforts and of which includes labeling victims denied Constitutional, Civil and Human Rights, as again Domestic Terrorist, or approval founded also on the Warrantless Spy Program. The issue is that these operations do not want victims before any judge unless they have successfully mentally programmed the victim of their wrong doing by repetitive degrading comments, breaking the victim then controlling the victim by the technological advancement.

Get the picture.

In order to get this type of Electronic Surveillance / fusion center testing programs in place, approval was passed from the Department of Defense to the Department of Homeland Security and to the Department of Justice to bring in advanced technology now in the hands of local police, Counter-terrorism divisions. The technology was once only available at FBI and higher levels, CIA and NSA, etc., and of course all branches of the military

Where does one go when men cross the line of ethics and morals under the law and resort to what is in reality, factual egregious criminal behavior themselves because of the ability to hide? Although my evidence was mounting, which included the voicemail recording, and a new hope of proving that the deterioration to my body, both hips, knees, and shoulder joints were happening by synthetic weapon means, using emergency room doctor documentation, it would still be a great challenge for me alone. Although I was now hopefully armed with what I again, naively hoped was substantiating evidence of physical torture, I knew that I would once again be up against the top guns in the legal field meaning federal, US, city or state attorneys and now specifically the military JAG.

Would the medical documentation prove that when the targeting of me by this technology began as attacks to my body which later built to the full crescendo of the pain attacks and extreme torture? Would the documentation prove that beforehand I was in relatively good shape as documented in my health records prior to?

The medical record documentation by doctors includes x-rays and lab results which proved my necessity later for two Total Hip Replacements, and that prior to I had only a mild case of osteoarthritis in one hip documented in 2005, and exacerbated quickly in 2010 of which I knew was by microwave directed energy weapon attacks and fully fledge effort around me. I knew this as accurate but proving it would become the issue not only for me but for the best attorney which would cost big dollars that conveniently most people targeted just do not have.

Of all the dangerous government surveillance powers that were expanded by the USA PATRIOT Act the National Security Letter (NSL) power under 18 U.S.C. § 2709 as expanded by PATRIOT, Section 505 is one of the most frightening and invasive.

These letters served on communications service providers like phone companies and ISPs allow the FBI to secretly demand data about ordinary American citizens' private communications and Internet activity without any meaningful oversight or prior judicial review. Recipients of NSLs are subject to a gag order that forbids them from ever revealing the letters' existence to their coworkers to their friends or even to their family members much less the public.

Law enforcement's systemic abuse of this power has been documented both by a Department of Justice investigations investigating itself, amusingly, and in documents obtained by the Electronic Frontier Foundation through a Freedom of Information Act request.

In April, 2008, the American Civil Liberties Union alleged that the military was using the FBI to skirt legal restrictions on domestic surveillance to obtain private records of Americans' Internet service providers, financial institutions and telephone companies.

The ACLU based its allegation on a review of more than 1,000 documents turned over to it by the Defense Department in response to a suit the rights group filed in 2007 for documents related to national security letters. The same month, the Electronic Frontier Foundation alleged that documents obtained from the FBI in response to its own Freedom of Information Act lawsuit showed that top FBI officials were aware of the bureau's misuse of national security letters for nearly two years before the misuse was reported.

Moreover, the government can obtain medical records containing private patient information. The government can also obtain records and lists of individuals who belong to political organizations if it believes the organization espouses political rhetoric contrary to the government. And there you have another terrorist label for approval.

The question then became could I prove that the escalated condition from mild, dormant osteoarthritis then in only one hip had been technologically progressed to extreme subsequent deterioration as necrosis or the hip killed by the microwave beam help me? It sure was worth another try.

Could the fact that my complaints and effort to document what was happening in my medical records and through x-rays help me after the x-rays factually revealed uncharacteristic damage?

Fortunately, it is a documented fact that the mild case of osteoarthritis of which I began with had been escalated to a condition called Avascular Necrosis. Avascular Necrosis or AVN is a disease where there is cellular death also known as necrosis of bone components due to interruption of the blood supply to a specific area. Basically, the microwave beam by consistent focus, in "The Program" and the operation center personnel joy of crippling as the watched and as their only measure of perceived control has repeatedly cooked the fluids out of the joint until it died.

A characteristic, of microwave human cooking weaponry is cooking by depleting the body or area by specific focused of natural fluids such as water and blood cooking it away. This is also as Peter Mooring describes, as like a piece of meat in a microwave oven calling it actually what is real is, people cooking.

Without blood, the bone tissue dies or necrosis results and the bone eventually collapse. If avascular necrosis involves the bones of a joint, studies proved that it often leads to destruction of the joint articular surfaces as is the case of the femoral head of hips.

There are many theories about what causes avascular necrosis. Some of the risk factors include chemotherapy, excessive steroid use, and post-trauma, such as a break for example. However, in the list, I had none of these causes. I had only systematic intentional deterioration which turned into AVN which never could have erupted from osteoarthritis beginnings.

The fact is that the deterioration to both of my hips joint advancing from osteoarthritis was a condition which could have lain dormant for years as osteoarthritis just did not happen. But sadly, don't try telling this to doctors, with rose colored glasses. Most never require hip replacement from osteoarthritis, if at all, until geriatric years.

In the medical profession, study after study reveals that osteoarthritis does not typically escalate into Avascular Necrosis. It is unheard of and a known fact. However, AVN can escalate to osteoarthritis but not vice versa.

In my case, Avascular Necrosis was not the originating condition for deterioration and bone necrosis.

So where did AVN or necrosis stem from? I knew it stemmed 100% from the nightly, repeated, relentless microwave directed energy weapon attacks and being told why and what they wanted from me through technological beamed harassment. I could feel the beam and also can feel it at this very moment penetrating my thigh muscle as I work on this book by the shift which came on at 10:00 p.m. to usually around 6:30 a.m. Two other noteworthy causes for AVN are alcoholism and more importantly, radiation.

Eight years ago, lab tests were documented in my medical records regarding my liver functioning as normal which if not, could have connected my hip deterioration to AVN. Avascular Necrosis can be caused through liver embolization due to alcoholism. However, my liver was documented as completely healthy and normal during lab tests during this time and after. I also stopped drinking altogether. I was fine and had only minor health issues prior to the targeting.

Another definite documented cause of AVN is radiation, whether non-ionizing, or ionizing. Non-ionizing is the type emitted from microwave directed energy weapons in the form of dielectric heating. The heating of my hip joint had caused AVN and it now appeared to be an aberration, which now also included the likelihood in the future for two knee replacements and loss of movement in my arms and my shoulders as the attacks persisted. If the beam is used to destroy areas all over my body, destroying my hip joints strategically revealed it would be done without the slightest of care.

In fact, these men are so evil that whereas they were once very verbal, due to these books, they are completely quiet now, and attacking my body without the combined verbal threats as I work knowing I will detail everything said for the public. They still are determined to destroy my body, but silently it appears illogically hoping I will not notice the unusual, uncharacteristic of the microwave pain slowly building in intensity as it had with both hip joints.

The depth of penetration depends on the frequency of the microwaves and the tissue.

The microwave directed energy weapon, which Nikola Tesla first called the "death ray" employs a microwave beam at 95 GHz; a two-second burst of the 95 GHz focused beam heats the skin to a temperature of 130 F (54 °C) at a depth of 1/64th of an inch (0.4 mm) and is claimed to cause skin pain without lasting damage. That is unless lasting damage is the desire.

Conversely, lower frequencies penetrate deeper; at 5.8 GHz the depth of most of the energy is dissipated in the first millimeter of the skin; the 2.45 GHz frequency microwaves commonly use. For example, a microwave oven can deliver energy deeper into the tissue. The generally accepted value is 17 mm for muscle tissue experts agree.

Lower frequencies, typical of extremely low frequency (ELF) technology and its effectiveness in electromagnetic weapons, are the pronounced effect when the energy penetrates deeper into the tissue. The damage occurs because there are only few nerve endings in deeper-located parts of the human tissue and the effects through the radio frequency waves as ELF. As a result, it is documented that the deterioration may not be immediately noticeable.

The lower frequencies, at ELF at high powered densities can be deadly. The human body acts as a broadband antenna with a number of resonation frequencies dictated by its size and position. The microwave absorption is directed and constant heating the tissue occurs. At 2.5 GHz, this ranges from about 5 for Adipose tissue. Adipose tissue is primarily located beneath the skin, but is also found around internal organs. In the integumentary system, which includes the skin, it accumulates in the deepest level, the subcutaneous layer, providing insulation from heat and cold. Around organs, it provides protective padding. It also functions as a reserve of nutrients.

The absorption is about 56 for the cardiac muscle. As the speed of electromagnetic waves is proportional to the reciprocal value of the square root of the dielectric or constant heating, the resulting wavelength in the tissue can drop to a fraction of the wavelength in air; e.g. at 10 GHz the wavelength can drop from 3 cm to about 3.4 mm. The layers of the body can be approximated as a thin layer of epidermis, dermis, adipose tissue (subcutaneous fat), and muscle tissue.

At dozens of gigahertz, the radiation is absorbed in the top fraction to top few millimeters of skin. Muscle tissue is a much more efficient absorber than fat, so lower frequencies can penetrate sufficiently deep and most energy gets deposited there. In a homogeneous medium, the energy/depth dependence is an exponential curve with the exponent depending on the frequency and tissue. For 2.5 GHz, the first millimeter of muscle tissue absorbs 11% of the heat energy the first two millimeters together absorb 20%. For lower frequencies, the attenuation factors are much lower, the achievable heating depths are higher, and the temperature gradient within the tissue is lower.

Microwave burns are very serious when caused by the thermal heating effects of non-ionizing radiation absorbed into living tissue. A microwave burn in comparison with burns caused by ionized radiation, where the dominant mechanism of tissue damage is internal cell damage is caused by free radicals. Free radicals damage DNA and cause cancer. Free radicals are highly reactive molecules that are produced in the body naturally as a byproduct of metabolism (oxidation), and by exposure to toxins in the environment such as tobacco smoke and ultraviolet light.

Microwave directed energy weapons are a form of ultraviolet light. Ultraviolet light or (UV) is a result of electromagnetic radiation. Free radicals contain an unpaired electron. Simply put, they are in a constant search to bond with another electron to stabilize them-- a process that can cause damage to DNA and other parts of human cells. This damage may play a role in the development of cancer and other diseases, and accelerate the aging process or death/necrosis. The primary damage mechanism of microwave radiation is thermal, or dielectric heating.

Perhaps most sinister in the use of this technology today is the fact that microwave deep tissue damage can manifest with delay, as pain and signs of skin damage show some time after microwave exposure thereby a "slow kill" affect.

At night, I could feel the beam deployed to the front part of my thighs, for example with slight discomfort as I lay on my back trying to sleep. The beam entered from the ceiling above me which again, indicates operation center drone directed. The pain was not enough to fully wake me but consciously noted as I tossed and turned. However, when I woke the next morning, movement accelerated the crippling effect immediately.

Exposure to frequencies common in domestic and industrial sources rarely leads to significant skin damage. In such cases, the damage tends to be limited to upper extremities. However, significant injury such as erythema, blisters, pain, nerve damage, and tissue necrosis can occur even with exposures as short as 2–3 seconds typical of the pain beam. Due to the deep penetration of these extremely low frequencies, the skin may be minimally affected and show no signs of damage, while within, muscles, nerves, and blood vessels may be significantly damaged.

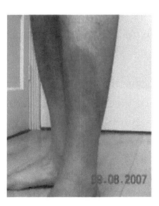

DEW hit August 9, 2007
This photo was taken August 9, 2007 after being burned day after day after day on the legs by a directed energy weapon (microwave weapon).
http://www.petermooring.nl

## Peter Mooring

Sensory nerves are particularly sensitive to such damage with documented cases of persistent neuritis and compression neuropathy being reported after significant microwave exposures.

When I started waking with numbness to only area left uncovered while sleeping, my hands and arms along with numbness I realized it would eventually possibly lead to nerve damage and they knew it too. My hands and arms suffered sporadic attacks, which also appeared to be an intense focus as I formulated this this book. Perhaps if in pain, I could not type they reasoned.

Microwave burns show similarities with electrical burns thus the term dielectric heating.

These deadly attacks to my body showed no mercy. Had they lingered with isolated focus to my eyes, the damage would be horrific so instead they hit my right eye sporadically as a form of slow deterioration. Cases of severe conjunctivitis were reported after technicians looked into powered waveguides. Microwave-induced cataract is also reported in partially documented cases. Some sources however mention incidence of microwave-related injuries of ocular lens and retina and the possibility of thermal effects to cause cataracts or focal tissue burns.

This knowledge is fully known in these programs by those directing this technology at a target or into an environment; community, group, or population, and these individuals are fully trained and well versed on how to use the technology, the anatomy and the end results. If there is no standard operating procedure, targets everywhere would not be reporting identical experiences across the board.

The psychotronic attacks are computer programs, so they follow identical "scripts" with accompanying identical physical effects.

Many people may claim of voices in their head, but, as with any crime, there is circumstantial evidence that is beyond coincidence as proof for the inquiring mind.

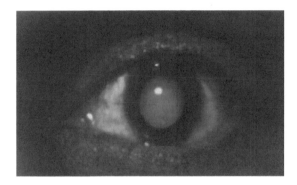

An example, and likely/possible result of the sporadic energy weapon beam's focus, set on a specific setting, targeting my eyes, could be technologically induced cataract.

After several treatments from the operation, and after the pain subsided the next morning, my vision was definitely blurred and there appeared to be a type of cloud formation obstructing my vision. Imagine repeated sporadic attacks making the condition appear as natural deterioration. Some sources mention incidence of microwave-related injuries of ocular lens and retina and the possibility of thermal effects to cause cataracts or focal tissue burns / damage including Keratitis.

A targeted individual wrote me telling me that one night he suffered a burning attack to his eyes and later he was informed during an eye exam that his 20/20 vision was no more.

# CHAPTER EIGHT
# Globalization

An excerpt from the website below is yet another effort by many, many other activists hoping to warn the public what is happening today. Make no mistake about it, if thousands of people the world over are reporting exact same experiences by advanced psychological electronic weapons, once known as mind control technology, and microwave Directed Energy Weapons, now in the forefront, and also reporting having both extreme physical and psychological experiences please take notice. We, victims of all races, appear to be the test subjects before full, total, complete, and extensive globalization likely to you and yours to insure total control.

In fact, prominent figures, not only in America, but also in the United Kingdom have actually made such claims of eventual total technocratic control of everyone on this planet.

Barrie Trower, of the United Kingdom retired from a position equivalent to the CIA there reported testing of entire communities as just one of the many facets of this technologies testing efforts of which he is quite familiar. This he reported is through firsthand knowledge and it being a definite globalized testing program as shown in the brief excerpt below:

M.I.5 Scientist "500,000 in UK Secret Experiment"

Retired MI5 officer Barry Trower reveals extensive new information about large scale experimentation via Porton Down, UK. He details the testing of psychotronic weapons on UK public and estimates eight or nine out of ten people involved are profoundly influenced as he describes experiments where these weapons have been tested on whole streets and describes how assassins are created. He estimates a success rate of around 80 - 90% in influencing and controlling people this way.

"I know that in one of the programs over a forty-year period, they took 500,000 people, I know that they had pregnant women, children over the age of 4, Catholics, Muslims, prisoners, drug addicts, service men."

It is the English government scientists, mainly from Porton Down, the big government military research center with total immunity from the law..." He writes.

Mr. Barrie Trower is a retired British physicist who was a microwave weapons expert who worked for the Royal Navy and the British Secret Service. He has come out of retirement with warnings and to alert the public both in the U.S. and the UK of the powerful capabilities of microwaves as a covert weapon and as a voice carrier of those operating it.

Today the voices of inmates saying it is happening to them are not being heard with no one really caring. They have been convicted and are paying for their crimes through the justice system but however are still valuable for human experimentation which in some cases landed them there in the first place.

Here is an excerpt from one person's experiences as a human lab rat inmate in the Utah prison system named David Fratus, in a letter written in October of 1988.

The link to his story in its entirety can be viewed at the link below the excerpt.

The letter proves ongoing human experimentation within the prison system.

I also believe that the prison system is also a location for emasculation of men beamed sexual stimulation and subliminal influence to create homosexuality. I often wonder why young black men have not a clue that "sagging" pants are a symbol of this. Yet, somehow in what appears to be a type of population mind control they believe it means Gangsta. The fact is, whomever coined the name, knew that sagging actually means niggas spelled backwards and it could likely be those at the helm of advance mind invasive mass subliminal influence systems. The hatred of some white men towards the black people, for no real justifiable reason could also be also the result of mass mind invasive technology influence and testing at a different level.

The various effects of this device have been progressively
increased throughout this eleven-month onslaught, finally
arriving at full potential with the end result being that I am
now having my brain monitored by an omnipotent computerized mind
reading or scanning machine of some sort. No hoax, no illusion to
what I'm experiencing. These people have devised or acquired a
specialized unit that reads absolutely everything--physical as
well as mental functions, and are able to cause severe
impairments and dysfunctions via this remote-control scanning
device. I have no memory of having had anything of a physical
nature done to me, but it has somehow been contrived to "wire" me
up to where they have access to instant, and unerringly accurate
comprehension of even my most fragmented and fleeting thoughts.
They are attempting radical behavior modification and thought
control by means of an incessant, round the clock monitoring of
my brain--imposing the various punishments when my thinking or
physical actions fail to conform to what they are demanding of
me. Interesting concept, isn't it? "Big Brother" and the "Thought
Police" have most assuredly become reality.

**Full Link to Story:** http://www.whale.to/b/fratus.html

It appears no one is exempt from testing and it appears necessary to understand the various useful affects in studies focused on "Remote Brain Targeting" and its technological effect on various people from different walks of life.

As I have mentioned, I personally had to move out of a neighborhood in Los Angeles. Because of my awareness and experiences with this technology and watching its use with clear eyes. I literally could see the whole neighborhood being manipulated and influenced and it not only sickened but the level of evil saddened me. I also recognized that people did not even have a clue about what was happening blatantly to them and right before their blinded hypnotic eyes.

In the corporate prison system, what better way to emasculate men than to lock them up, back up a powerful naturally occurring sexual urge, then implant thoughts of homosexuality, then combined the urge with actual physical electromagnetic sexual stimulation as stated.

And without a doubt is also being deployed into middle class white America too heinously. Again, no one appears to be exempt from what is happening today.

As part of this global agenda of which we've heard so much boast by the elite, it appears that depopulation is also high on the list. That which nourishes the human body for growth and development, our food is contaminated and lacks nourishment and is therefore contributing to dummying everyone.

While this cabal or so-call one percent, for example, has organically grown food, clear water and who, I can almost guarantee would never drink water contaminated by fluoride which is the equivalent of arsenic and a derivative of aluminum.

They also, I am sure, live in Chemtrail free air filtered businesses and homes.

Expert after expert continues their warnings of electromagnetic technology usage and the effect on the environment overall:

We are now living under daily radiation, chemical and biological siege. Because so much of this is invisible, it may be difficult for many people to comprehend the enormity of what is happening throughout our environment. The on-going catastrophe at Japan's Fukushima ruined nuclear reactors continues to affect our entire planet. From the very beginning and behind the scenes of this epic crisis, the real reasons were deliberately covered-up. Safety factors were omitted; citizens continue to be put in harm's way in Japan, throughout North America, and the rest of the planet. Mainstream Orwellian news is worthless in terms of reporting the magnitude and real dangers involved; so, the public has never been properly informed. As with the on-going BP Gulf of Mexico oil-rig catastrophe, all we get as citizens are distortions and deception. Safe ways of handling this nightmare or real precaution were deliberately not part of any "emergency" plan.

We have a long-term planetary-wide epic tragedy unfolding. It is the most serious man-made catastrophe that we have faced in our human history.

We are all being assaulted on several fronts with a three-pronged attack:

(1) a decades-long hazardous brew of daily Chemtrails battering that is affecting our entire biosphere;

(2) long-term and very dangerous ionizing radiation exposure, with Fukushima as a new and critically toxic addition; and

(3) the release of Nano-bioweapons into our environment…

writes Dr. Ilya Sandra - The Worldwide Environmental Crisis Gone Missing: The Precautionary Principle"

Today, not only critical thinkers, but many believe that there appears to a decisive agenda to affect any possible fighting spirit of protest from humanity, or to alert humanity with a growing catastrophe, by not only pharmaceutical medications, but street drugs, that have been introduced into middle class America heavily as opiates pain killers and Heroin.

What if the addiction, which typically works hand in hand with historic mind control programming and programs were then followed up with extremely low frequency population control through the effective manipulation of your consciousness and perception?

Some in the targeted community have been nudged into drug use. Due to debilitating pain, those in the operation center I can attest would have loved it if I became addicted to pain medication and I heard it mentioned once a few years back.

Heroin, Crystal Meth, and Crack Cocaine, which the poor are not bringing into this country, has quietly reached epidemic proportions in many communities to include rural communities across America today without exception and continues to destroy whole generations of all races.

Most do not know that one of the evilest regimes in history, Hitler's Nazi regime, actually utilized Crystal Meth for troop manipulation and motivation and to keep soldiers robotized and controlled in order to do Nazi bidding. Hitler had meth laced chocolates created for his military personnel and was reportedly an addict himself. Special ones were made just for flyers and tank drivers.

Globalization was the motivating force then as is also now it by escalated determination.

Historically, drugs, both pharmaceutical and street drugs have been very effectively used as one of the most prolific sources of human control on a widespread level and continues to play a very important and major role today as a form of mind control to include profitable on many levels for the global Elite creating wars and exporting the spoils of war. In fact, U.S. troops are documented in images guarding opium fields in Afghanistan.

We are in the Police State as result of a belief that many are expendable or marginal or what the movie "Toxic Skies" calls useless, worthless food eaters. Interestingly this perception believed held by secret societies, which we are told are leading the pack, has traditionally based their esoteric knowledge and studies on ancient knowledge and practices originating in Ancient Egypt. The doctrine of Freemasonry incorporates Egyptian symbolism into various stages of their rituals.

Studies show that a psychopath is not really that intelligent. What they are is emotionally intelligent. They are very good at reading people, dotting their "I's" and crossing their "T's". They are good at manipulating the emotions of people for their own good or benefit and can be deadly.

Today we are dealing with a global system, and the egotistical agenda of a small group, we call the global Elite. It appears this minority is decisively bent on decades of harnessing the free energy of the universe for their own nefarious goals, control, needs, and bad deeds.

Many targets understand more so than many that these weapons, consciousness altering, and the telepathic technology weapon system are here to stay. From our extensive experience, we also understand also that this situation is a Goliath to conquer and destroy yet we persist through information.

Make no mistake about it, the next generation of brainwashing began almost immediately with many saying, including one of the ladies visiting me from North California, that she believes she has been targeted since birth and she is now in her late-40s.

Another whistleblower, and also a prominent targeted individual has been whistleblowing for quite some time and writes:

The U.S. government is systematically assaulting, torturing, and impairing thousands of extra judicially "targeted individuals" with a cellular electromagnetic radio frequency weapon system that is hiding in plain sight.

It may have started out using existing GWEN towers, but that was just the roll-out for the Delta-T form factor phased array antenna scalar electromagnetic weapon installation that's atop of cellular towers. The weapon system is housed on cellular towers proprietary to the weapon system, and, in some locations, is apparently co-located with consumer cellphone antennae. When I first wrote about "Delta T," the censorship regime removed the references and I had to keep putting the information back into my main story (see U.S. Silently Tortures Americans with Cell Tower Electromagnetic Weapon at http://viclivingston.blogspot.com/2011/12/u.html). And there was no mention that MULTIPLE antennas are used to "triangulate" targets, in the same manner that a cellphone signal is delivered to a geo-specific device...

The example below depicts the capability of satellite delivered synthetic telepathy via satellite back to a ground station then to a target. What is not shown is also the similar capability of deployment of directed energy weapons through communication towers directly to a target also.

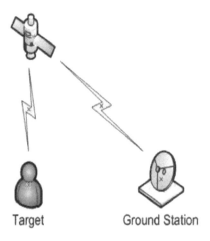

Target          Ground Station

The Microwave Hum or Sonic Weapon

Could ELF waves generated by HAARP be what are causing the weird noise as a humming sound being heard around the world?

Depending on your location, you may have heard the noise as well. People in Texas, Philadelphia, Vancouver, Brazil, Madrid, Germany, Russia, Hawaii and more, have all recorded and reported hearing these noises recently. The question is, what would cause these deep hums and odd harmonic noises?

There are 84 registered FCC microwave towers near my home alone. However, bear in mind, that not all towers must be registered with the FCC so there could be more. And, we're talking within a one to three-mile radius of me. This is also nationwide.

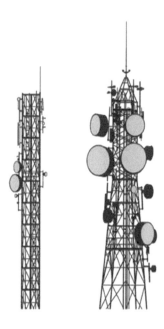

Not only in America are we dealing with this global system in many forms, but as shown by the article below, people all over the world are experiencing some residual effects of microwave radio frequencies, however, many do not have a clue what is happening, how or why, much less it being even possible:

Mysterious hum driving people crazy around the world by Marc Lallanilla - Live Science

The article begins by saying, "It's known as the Hum, a steady, droning sound that's heard in places as disparate as Taos, N.M.; Bristol, England; and Largs, Scotland…"

Directed energy weapons include lasers, high power microwave, and millimeter wave models among others. A relevant December 2007 Department of Defense (DOD) report called them a "transformational game changer in military operations, able to augment and improve operational capabilities in many areas," for both lethal and non-lethal purposes.

Sonic Weapons under the heading of Directed Energy Weapons on Wikipedia states that the auditory effect causes deathly symptoms such as:

1. Cavitation, which affects gas nuclei in human tissue, and heating can result from exposure to ultrasound and can damage tissue and organs. Studies have found that exposure to high intensity ultrasound at frequencies from 700 kHz to 3.6 MHz can cause lung and intestinal damage in mice. Heart rate patterns following vibro-acoustic stimulation have resulted in serious arterial flutter and bradycardia. Researchers have concluded that generating pain through the auditory system using high intensity sound risked permanent hearing damage.

2. A multi-organization research program involved high intensity audible sound experiments on human subjects. Extra-aural (unrelated to hearing) bio-effects on various internal organs and the central nervous system included auditory shifts, vibro-tactile sensitivity change, muscle contraction, cardiovascular function change, central nervous system effects, vestibular (inner ear) effects, and chest wall /lung tissue effects. Researchers found that low frequency sonar exposure could result in significant cavitations, hypothermia and tissue shearing. Follow-on experiments were not recommended.

3. Tests performed on mice show the threshold for both lung and liver damage occurs at about 184 dB. Damage increases rapidly as intensity is increased. Noise-induced Neurological disturbances in humans exposed to continuous low frequency tones for durations longer than 15 minutes involved development of immediate and long-term problems affecting brain tissue. The symptoms resembled those of individuals who had suffered minor head injuries. One theory for a causal mechanism is that the prolonged sound exposure resulted in enough mechanical strain to brain tissue to induce an encephalopathy. After they finished the three 15 minute's

treatments I received as I worked, I was left shaken with a weird sensation in my head with sharp pains, my nervous system obviously rattled.

In this brief excerpt, first published by Global Research in June of 2004 entitled, Chemtrails: Aerosol and Electromagnetic Weapons in the Age of Nuclear War by Amy Worthington, Global Research, March 23, 2013, it states that:

North America is now suffering its seventh year of conspicuous and dangerous aerosol and electromagnetic operations conducted by the U.S. government under the guise of national security. Concerned citizens watch in fear as military tankers discolor the skies with toxic chemicals that morph into synthetic clouds.

We continually witness bizarre meteorological occurrences as powerful electromagnetic devices manipulate both the jet stream and individual storm fronts to create artificial weather and climatic conditions. Black operations projects embedded within these aerosol missions are documented to sicken and disorient select populations with biological test agents and psychotronic mind/mood control technologies.

The report goes on to say,

Part of what is happening in the atmosphere above us involves the Pentagon's secret space weapons program, designed for strategic, operational and tactical levels of war. NASA missions will soon be transferred to Pentagon control.

1. The Air Force Space Command declares that, in order to monitor and shape world events, it must fight intense, decisive wars with great precision from space.
2. Air Force Secretary James G. Roche has stated: "Space capabilities are integrated with, and affect every link in the kill chain."

3. A glimpse into new death technologies under construction is in legislation introduced by Ohio Congressman Dennis Kucinch. His unsuccessful Space Preservation Act of 2001 was intended to ban space deployment of:

* electronic, psychotronic and information weaponry* high altitude ultra-low frequency weapons

* plasma, electromagnetic, sonic and ultrasonic weapons

* laser weapons

* strategic, theater, tactical or extraterrestrial weapons

* chemical biological, environmental climate or tectonic weapons

* chemtrails (this item was stricken from a later version, suggesting duress).

Silly me, I moved outside of Los Angeles, to the desert near one of the largest Air Forces bases in the country and one of the lead microwave Directed Energy Weapon contractors. I have personally witnessed numerous air crafts spraying then the next day the desert weather becomes cloudy and even at time rains in late July and August, which are the hottest days of the year in the desert.

USAF Weather Modification Program

The Evergreen Air fleet of 747 Tankers patented for Weather Modification are capable of deploying aerosols that fit the description of "Chembombs"

# CHAPTER NINE
# Conclusion

DHS 'fusion centers' portrayed as pools of ineptitude, civil liberties intrusions, writes Robert O' Harrow Jr., October 2, 2012

An initiative aimed at improving intelligence sharing has done little to make the country more secure, despite as much as $1.4 billion in federal spending, according to a two-year examination by Senate investigators…" The report begins.

Disenchantment continues to rise as listed below:

1. Rand Paul, R-Kentucky, Homeland Security Subcommittee on Emergency Management – Ranking Member is on the record saying that "The problem with fusion centers is that they have targeted people based on political beliefs."

   http://www.youtube.com/watch?v=8_NkJZd5cWY&feature =youtube_gdata_player_

2. Senator Wyden, Surveillance, Security and Privacy, Center for American Progress Action Fund, Washington, D.C., "Warns the US Could Become a "Surveillance State" With Government Monitoring Your Every Move!" –

   See more at:
   http://xrepublic.tv/node/4561#sthash.v6Hp5pVi.dpuf

3. Tim Shorrock, Author, "Spies for Hire," Spying on Americans is a big business / Private contractor run US intelligence

See more at: http://www.brasschecktv.com/videos/the-surveillance-state/spying-on-americans-is-a-big-business.html#sthash.DOZygriY.dpuf

4. "Corporate America Is Using Our Police Departments as Hired Thugs" Ret Police Captain Ray Lewis

http://www.youtube.com/watch?feature=player_detailpage&v=wdkd2adjjUw

5. Homeland Security 'fusion' centers spy on citizens, produce 'shoddy' work, report says by Ranking Republican on Senate panel, Sen. Tom Coburn of Oklahoma. By Michael Isikoff, NBC News Investigations, October 2, 2012

http://investigations.nbcnews.com/_news/2012/10/02/14187433-homeland-security-fusion-centers-spy-on-citizens-produce-shoddy-work-report-says?lite

Ex FBI decorated agent, Mike German, and ACLU attorney explains in a series of you tube videos how the national security state, is now fully integrated into a larger political secret police apparatus. He also connects the dots in areas such as Gang Stalking and injustice at the FBI through Electronic Harassment Surveillance, technology and the Police State.

Today, bogus investigations are being used to open the door for placement into "The Program." They are bogus because many victims have been in this program since early childhood.

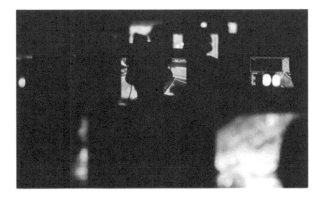

The goal is to use electromagnetic technology to brainwash or coerce a person into a belief of wrongdoing through a type of electromagnetic hypnosis using several black bag technologies, or sadly misconstruing of sub-vocal thought as foundation for targeting and torture or death. If the effort fails, and a person becomes a threat in any way, such as book exposure for example, slow kill technology can be deployed because some perceive human life valueless by a certain standard and individuals are being paid specifically to do this type of employment and will stretch the limits in order to preserve the secrecy of what they are doing.

**Excerpts in the ACLU report continue to reveal that:**

The American Civil Liberties Union also issued a statement saying the report underscores problems that it and other civil liberty groups have been flagging for years. "The ACLU warned back in 2007 that fusion centers posed grave threats to Americans' privacy and civil liberties, and that they needed clear guidelines and independent oversight," said Michael German, ACLU senior policy counsel. "This report is a good first step, and we call upon Congress to hold public hearings to investigate fusion centers and their ongoing abuses."

**Reports of fraud, waste and abuse are documented with another report stating that:**

In addition to the value of much of the fusion centers' work, the Senate panel found evidence of what it called "troubling" reports by some centers that may have violated the civil liberties and privacy of U.S. citizens. The evidence cited in the report could fuel a continuing controversy over claims that the FBI and some local police departments, notably New York City's, have spied on American Muslims without a justifiable law enforcement reason for doing so. Among the examples in the report:

- One fusion center drafted a report on a list of reading suggestions prepared by a Muslim community group, titled "Ten Book Recommendations for Every Muslim." The report noted that four of the authors were listed in a terrorism database, but a Homeland Security reviewer in Washington chastised the fusion center, saying, "We cannot report on books and other writings" simply because the authors are in a terrorism database. "The writings themselves are protected by the First Amendment unless you can establish that something in the writing indicates planning or advocates violent or other criminal activity."

- A fusion center in California prepared a report about a speaker at a Muslim center in Santa Cruz who was giving a daylong motivational talk—and a lecture on "positive parenting." No link to terrorism was alleged.

- Another fusion center drafted a report on a U.S. citizen speaking at a local mosque that speculated that -- since the speaker had been listed in a terrorism data base — he may have been attempting "to conduct fundraising and recruiting" for a foreign terrorist group.

Also, in another excerpt from this report:

The report cited multiple examples of what fusion center reports that had little if any value to counterterrorism efforts.

One fusion center report cited described how a certain model car had folding rear seats to the trunk, a feature that it said could be useful to human traffickers. This prompted a Homeland Security reviewer to note that such folding rear seats are "featured on many different makes and model of vehicles" and "there is nothing of any intelligence value in this report."

Another fusion center report, entitled "Possible Drug Smuggling Activity," recounted the experiences of two state wildlife officials who spotted a pair of men in a bass boat "operating suspiciously" in the body of water off the U.S.-Mexico border. The report noted that the fishermen "avoided eye contact" and that their boat appeared to be low in the water, "as if it was laden with cargo" with high winds and choppy waters.

"The fact that some guys were hanging out in a boat where people normally do not fish MIGHT be an indicator of something abnormal, but does not reach the threshold of something we should be reporting," a Homeland Security reviewer wrote, according to the Senate panel. "I ... think that this should never have been nominated for production, nor passed through three reviews."

Getting to the bottom of who, what, where and why continues to be one of the greatest challenges facing Targeted Individuals through an intentional shrouding of layers of involvement by numerous agencies or many operating together thus the term Fusion.

One thing is certain; this is 100% "The Program" is a definite reality.

Tim Shorrock mentioned the involvement of government contractors. One contractor, beyond a shadow of a doubt is a high stakes player in the role of microwave directed energy weapon technology, along with others such as Raytheon is Lockheed Martin.

In 2010, reports surfaced that Lockheed Martin had been given the contract and would be developing a new weapon for the United States Air Force that uses microwaves to destroy (cook?) electronic targets.

Thousands of thoughts run through the mind each day. This figure is based on information from UCLA study, which states that the average person has 70,000 thoughts per day. If we divide that amount by 24 hours and then by 60 minutes per hour, we get the figure of 48.61 thoughts per minute. This fact alone makes the ability for humans to read another person's thought and draw conclusions then use the information to hurt or harm a person horrendously unjust especially when based on sub-vocal thought deciphering another reason exposure is not wanted.

So now that you are aware of this crazy technology, perhaps a tin foil hat is not out of the question or a joke anymore, in the Matrix.

I and others have learned, regarding deflective and protective material, that those deploying the energy weapon system simply turn the power up to the next or higher setting. The search continues for effective deflection from the beamed assaults.

And understand that much of what is happening today, for example, mind reading technology has been around for decades and studies began with the invention of the Electroencephalogram in the 1920s which eventually led up to the use of highly advanced brainwave analyzing technology today. And as revealed at the beginning of this book is antediluvian. Most of the information below is nothing new to victims of targeting operations forced to research. The hope is to bring the knowledge into the public domain.

Brainwave monitors / analyzers / mind thought deciphering technology

Lawrence Pinneo, a neurophysiologist and electronic engineer working for Stanford Research Institute (a military contractor) is the first "known" pioneer in this field. In 1974, he developed a computer system which correlated brain waves on an electroencephalograph with specific commands.

In the early 1990s, Dr. Edward Taube reported that words could be communicated onto a screen using the thought-activated movements of the computer cursor.

## How is it done?

The magnetic field around the head, the brain waves of an individual can be monitored by satellite. The transmitter is therefore the brain itself just as body heat is used for "Iris" satellite tracking (infrared) or mobile phones or bugs can be tracked as "transmitters." In the case of the brain wave monitoring the results are then fed back to the relevant computers. Monitors then use the information to conduct "conversation" where audible Neurophone (a form of synthetic telepathy using the nervous system) input is "applied" to the target / victim.

### Brainwave Scanners / Programs

First program developed in 1994 by Dr. Donald York and Dr. Thomas Jensen.

In 1994, the brain wave patterns of 40 subjects were officially correlated with both spoken words and silent thought. This was achieved by a neurophysiologist, Dr. Donald York, and a speech pathologist, Dr. Thomas Jensen, from the University of Missouri. They clearly identified 27 words, / syllables in specific brain wave patterns and produced a computer program with a brain wave vocabulary

Using lasers / satellites, and high-powered computers, the agencies have now gained the ability to decipher human thoughts - and from a considerable distance, instantaneously.

DESCRIPTION: As personal scanning and tracking system involving the monitoring of an individual EMF via remote means; e.g. Satellite. The results are fed to thought activated computers that possess a complete brainwave vocabulary.

PURPOSE: Practically, communication with stroke victims and brain-activated control of modern jets are two applications. However, more often, it is used to mentally rape a Civilian target; their thoughts being referenced immediately and/ or recorded for future use.

## EEG CLONING

Description: A system whereby the target's EMF is monitored remotely and EEG results fed back to them (or others) to mimic emotional patterns; e.g. fear, anger, etc...

Purpose: To induce emotional / psychological responses. For example, the feedback of Delta waves may induce drowsiness since these are familiar when in deep sleep.

This entire bracket of weapons was referred to by L. Brezhnev in 1978 when he told then U.S. President J. Carter that there should be a unilateral ban on certain secret weapons "more frightful than the mind of man has ever conceived." And clearly there are many others that we are yet to learn about; including advanced forms of infrasound weapons that can induce organ damage/illness from remote sources (esp. satellites).

The combined use of several technologies enables remote torture and interrogation. (Memories are triggered by Neurophone questioning and the brain wave analyzers deliver the answer.) Any nebulous arguments about U.S. national security and the need for classified research on human subjects speak for themselves.

The three most commonly used psychological technologies of today within the Targeted Individual community are

(1) the technological telepathy effect also known as patented subliminal or hearing voices effect, being used to discredit people as delusional or psychotic and schizophrenic

(2) EEG cloning and thought deciphering being used to electronic harass you with sub-vocal thought

(3) Directed Energy Weapon coercive torture

Of the three I personally find the EEG cloning to the most unethical and immoral. It is imperative to grasp mood alteration.

Those in operation centers sit and listen to your irrelevant thoughts all day long, trying to create fear, and play back to you your sub-vocal thoughts all day long. If you believe them when they are constantly repeating these things back to you, that may have crossed your mind, you have been effectively mind controlled by their mimicking.

Control can also be accomplished by using repetitive threats of your demise, whereas the operation has also recorded and registered your emotions and especially fear. When you experience fear, or any other useful emotions for their targeting use such as anger, or sadness as well, remember that the emotion is duplicated and placed into a super computer brain interface and beamed back to you and resonates to your personal biometric signature which is essentially your brain's personal finger print. Those in the operation center then use your cloned emotions against you when electronically harassing you lowering your frequency too an immediate mood switch for example from peace and calm to sadness, aggression and more. For example, after you are repeatedly told you are getting ready to die, the cloned and previously recorded emotion is played back to you using the fear they have stored to emotionally shake you up negatively. These operations are not in the business for creating positive energy, joy or happiness.

You can experience crippling fear and depression from EEG cloned emotions. When you succumb, you are thereby controlled. The key is knowledge and awareness!

As I stated earlier, rest assured that they cannot tap into the sacred place within you where absolute truth lies with their so called and synthetic computer cloning technology and manipulative games which they try and try to penetrate with many of the tougher targets. Do not let them convince you of their objective, as they play back to you that which you have not verbalized to yourself as a genuine conclusion or suggestions which they have transformed from their voice into yours and beamed.

As I wrapped up this book, they again verbalized the same threat, also said after completion of the first two books that has always been the foundation for escalation and the continued slow kill attempted murder around, my life in a program most have suffered up to the grave, sooner or later.

Typically, one of them said, "that book" meaning this new one, just before excruciating torture was unleashed to insure I got the message.

While finishing this manuscript, I began to wake each morning to begin working; with both hands completely numb. Before I got out of bed and to insure the numbness was their doing, I covered my hands and arms under the rubber mat protective material I was sleeping under and I could feel the blood flow returning to normal.

The question is, has our government, literally, created human monsters and official cold-blooded killers? It appears so.

"It's time for me to get to work" one said as he slid into his seat at his work station in the beamed effortlessly into my home office from the operation center, around 3:30 p.m. beginning the shift usually working until approximately 10:30 p.m. at night

"Ditto," I replied in thought, "It's time for me to get to work also."

His work was torturing me and others to a slow and painful death, of which he proudly boasted with joy in his voice. My work had inadvertently become and activist and exposing them and frankly it was greatly awarding to me and in and of itself alleviated a lot of the physical pain.

The End or a Beginning of Awareness?

# MISCELLANEOUS IMAGES

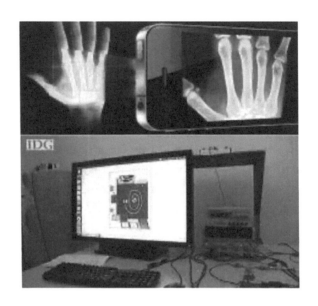

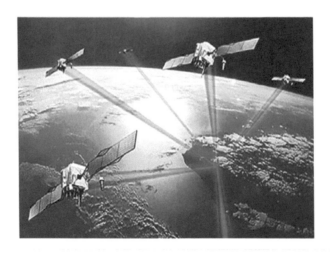

1990: US Patent # 4959559 – Electromagnetic or other directed energy pulse launcher

Background of the Invention – 4959559

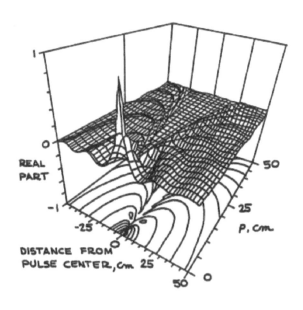

Bofors HPM Blackout

## *Active Denial System (ADS) 1 & 2*

System 1

System 2

| | |
|---|---|
| **Status:** Prototype<br>**Lead Agency:** JNLWD | |
| **Target Type:** Counter-Personnel | |
| **Intended Target Response:** Deny access into/out of an area to individuals, move individuals through an area, and suppress individuals. | |
| **Description:** Long range, directed energy, vehicle mounted system that projects an invisible electromagnetic millimeter-wave energy beam beyond small arms range. | |

**Concept of Employment:** Force protection, entry control points, and other offensive and defensive operations.

**Capability Effect:** Heat sensation causing involuntary movement away from the beam.

## *(U) ADS 1 & 2 cont.*

Heat Effect to Individuals
(U)

(U) **Delivery System:** Vehicle or ground mounted.

(FOUO) **Collateral Damage:** Potential for minor burns if over exposed.

(FOUO) **Counter Measures:** Cover and barriers, such as walls/buildings.

(FOUO) **Environmental Effects:** Rain and humidity may degrade effects.

(U) **Policy Implications:** See NLW Policy References (Active Denial System).

(U) **Unique Logistics:** None

## *Improved Acoustic Hailing Device (IAHD)*

**Anticipated Fielding:** FY12
**Status:** Developmental
**Lead Agency:** USA

**Target Type:** Counter-Personnel

**Intended Target Response:** Deny access into/out of an area to individuals, move individuals through an area, and suppress individuals.

**Description:** A long range hailing and warning device capable of producing directional sound beams to project warning tones and improved intelligible voice commands with background noise present at the target's location. Maximum Effective Range is 300 m threshold/1000 m objective.

**Concept of Employment:** Force protection, convoys, checkpoints, port operations to warn/hail individuals.

**Capabilities Effect:** Auditory impairment and/or intelligible audible tones.

## *Improved Acoustic Hailing Device (IAHD)*

**Anticipated Fielding:** FY12
**Status:** Developmental
**Lead Agency:** USA

**Target Type:** Counter-Personnel

**Intended Target Response:** Deny access into/out of an area to individuals, move individuals through an area, and suppress individuals.

**Description:** A long range hailing and warning device capable of producing directional sound beams to project warning tones and improved intelligible voice commands with background noise present at the target's location. Maximum Effective Range is 300 m threshold/1000 m objective.

**Concept of Employment:** Force protection, convoys, checkpoints, port operations to warn/hail individuals.

**Capabilities Effect:** Auditory impairment and/or intelligible audible tones.

## *Non-Lethal Unmanned Aerial Vehicle (UAV) High Power Microwave (HPM) Payload*

**Status:** Conceptual
**Lead Agency:** JNLWD

**Target Type:** Counter-Materiel

**Intended Target Response:** Stop or disable vessels.

**Description:** Develop an aerially deliverable high power microwave payload providing a long range non-lethal capability for small vessel stopping, swarm defense and ship system disruption.

**Concept of Employment:** Force protection, port operations, and vessel pursuit/stop/interdiction.

**Capability Effect:** Stops vessel propulsion by electrical system malfunction.

## *RF Vessel Stopper*

**Status:** Conceptual
**Lead Agency:** JNLWD

**Target Type:** Counter-Materiel

**Intended Target Response:** Stop or disable vessels.

**Description:** Develop stationary or mobile high power microwave payload providing a long range non-lethal capability for small vessel stopping, swarm defense and ship system disruption.

**Concept of Employment:** Force protection, port operations, and vessel pursuit/stop/interdiction.

**Capability Effect:** Stops vessel propulsion by electrical system malfunction.

## *Airborne Active Denial*

**Status:** Conceptual
**Lead Agency:** USAF Service Unique

**Target Type:** Counter-Personnel

**Intended Target Response:** Deny access into/out of an area to individuals, move individuals through an area, and suppress individuals.

**Description:** Directed energy system on a fixed-wing platform with operationally significant range and standoff.

**Concept of Employment:** Force protection, crowd control, detainee operations, patrols/convoys, building clearing, and other offensive and defensive operations.

**Capability Effect:** Heat sensation causing involuntary movement away from the beam.

## *Laser Based Flow Modification*

**Status:** Conceptual
**Lead Agency:** JNLWD

**Target Type:** Counter-Materiel

**Intended Target Response:** Divert aircraft from restricted area.

**Description:** A laser-based approach to modify the flow across control surfaces of an airplane. This effect is achieved by directing a pulsed laser at the leading edge of the airfoil in order to adjust the drag and lift on a plane, externally controlling the steering forces through modifying aerodynamic flow.

**Concept of Employment:** Divert aircraft from restricted area.

**Capabilities Effect:** Force aircraft to divert from path by modifying airflow across control surfaces.

## *Compact Active Denial Technologies (ADT)*

**Status:** Conceptual
**Lead Agency:** JNLWD

**Target Type:** Counter-Personnel

**Intended Target Response:** Deny access into/out of an area to individuals, move individuals through an area, and suppress individuals.

**Description:** A next generation tube-based ADT system that will drastically reduce size, weight, cost, and allow for instant "turn-on" and "shoot-on-the-move" capabilities.

**Concept of Employment:** Force protection, crowd control, patrols/convoys, and other defensive and offensive operations.

**Capability Effect:** Heat sensation causing involuntary movement away form the beam.

## Solid State Active Denial Technology (ADT)

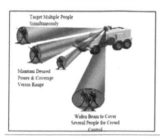

**Status:** Conceptual
**Lead Agency:** USA

**Target Type:** Counter-Personnel

**Intended Target Response:** Deny access into/out of an area to individuals, move individuals through an area, and suppress individuals.

**Description:** Solid state will yield a more compact system by combining the functionality of the existing ADT gyrotron, antenna, sub-reflector, and beam transport into a single unit that will drastically reduce size, weight, and cost.

**Concept of Employment:** Force protection, crowd control, detainee operations, patrols/convoys, building clearing, and other offensive and defensive operations.

**Capability Effect:** Heat sensation causing involuntary movement away from the beam.

## Ocular Interruption (OI)

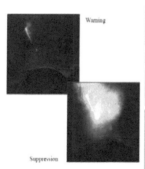

**Anticipated Fielding:** FY14
**Status:** Developmental
**Lead Agency:** USMC Service Unique

**Target Type:** Counter-Personnel

**Intended Target Response:** Deny access into/out of an area to individuals, move individuals through an area, and suppress individuals.

**Description:** A light emitting, non-damaging, eye-safe device to warn (primary) and suppress (secondary) individuals with 10-500 m standoff. This device will be a visible laser or high powered broad band lamp designed to maximize range while minimizing nominal ocular hazard distance.

**Concept of Employment:** Escalation of force continuum options during force protection, entry control points, checkpoints, convoys, and maritime ports and security zones.

**Capability Effect:** Optical impairment.

## *(U) OI cont.*

| |
|---|
| (U) **Delivery Systems:** Handheld or weapon mounted. |
| (FOUO) **Collateral Damage:** Potential for eye damage if exposed within Nominal Ocular Hazard Distance. |
| (FOUO) **Counter Measures:** Filtering goggles. |
| (FOUO) **Environmental Effects:** Reduced effect during daylight, fog, and rain. During daylight-moderate glare, no flash blindness, some afterimage. |
| (U) **Policy Implications:** See NLW Policy References (Optical Distractors). |
| (U) **Unique Logistics:** None |

## *Green Lasers*

| |
|---|
| **Currently fielded by USA, USMC, USN, and USAF:** COTS items, result of Urgent Needs Statement (UNS). **Lead Agency:** USMC |
| **Target Type:** Counter-Personnel |
| **Intended Target Response:** Deny access into/out of an area to individuals, move individuals through an area, and suppress individuals. |

| |
|---|
| **Description:** The LA-9/P™ has a maximum output of 250 mW and has an integrated Safety Control Module (SCM) that shuts the beam off when an object interrupts the beam within the 0-65 m Nominal Ocular Hazard Distance (NOHD). The LA-9/P™ has a range of 65 - 1000 m. The GLARE® MOUT is smaller and has a maximum output of 125 mW and a NOHD of 18 m. The GLARE® MOUT has a range of 18 - 760 m. |
| **Concept of Employment:** Force protection, entry control points, checkpoints, and maritime ports and security zones to warn, deny, move, and suppress (e.g., distract, disorient, and degrade) individuals on foot and those operating vehicles/vessels. |
| **Capability Effect:** Ocular impairment. |

## (U) Green Lasers cont.

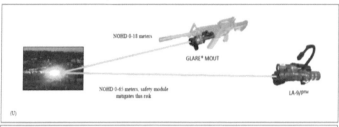

NOHD 0-18 meters

GLARE® MOUT

NOHD 0-65 meters, safety module
mitigates this risk

LA-9/P™

(U)

| | |
|---|---|
| (U) **Delivery Systems:** Hand held, mounted on a rifle or crew served weapon. | |
| (FOUO) **Collateral Damage:** Potential for eye damage if exposed within the NOHD. | |
| (FOUO) **Counter Measures:** Filtering goggles. | |
| (FOUO) **Environmental Effects:** Reduced effect during fog and rain. During daylight-moderate glare, no flash blindness, some afterimage. | |
| (U) **Policy Implications:** See NLW Policy References (Optical Distractors). | |
| (U) **Unique Logistics:** None | |

## Green Laser Interdiction System (GLIS)

**Anticipated Fielding:** FY12
**Status:** Developmental
**Lead Agency:** USA Service Unique

**Target Type:** Counter-Personnel

**Intended Target Response:** Deny access into/out of an area to individuals, move individuals through an area, and suppress individuals.

**Description:** The GLIS is a rifle-mounted/hand-held laser that allows interdiction of potential hostile actions through non-lethal effects and interchangeable between host weapon platforms. Effective non-lethal means to inform civilians they are approaching military operations with visible effects 0-300 m.

**Concept of Employment:** Force protection, entry control points, checkpoints, and maritime ports and security zones to warn, deny, move, and suppress (e.g., distract, disorient, and degrade) individuals on foot and those operating vehicles/vessels.

**Capability Effect:** Ocular impairment.

# (U) GLIS cont.

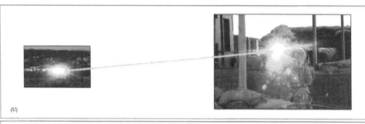

(U)

| (U) **Delivery Systems:** Handheld, mounted on a rifle or crew served weapon. |
| (FOUO) **Collateral Damage:** Potential for eye damage if exposed within the NOHD. |
| (FOUO) **Counter Measures:** Filtering goggles. |
| (FOUO) **Environmental Effects:** Reduced effect during fog and rain. During daylight - moderate glare, no flash blindness, some afterimage. |
| (U) **Policy Implications:** See NLW Policy References (Optical Distractors). |
| (U) **Unique Logistics:** None |

# Long Range Ocular Interruption (LROI)

**Anticipated Fielding:** TBD
**Status:** Developmental
**Lead Agency:** USN

**Target Type:** Counter-Personnel

**Intended Target Response:** Deny access into/out of an area to individuals, move individuals through an area, and suppress individuals.

**Description:** Optical interruption device delivering a visible spectrum, non-lethal, long range, reversible effect for counter-personnel applications for hailing, warning, and suppression in protection of Military High Value Assets (HVAs). LROI will manage NOHD at various ranges and have an effective range up to 3000 m.

**Concept of Employment:** Escalation of force continuum options during force protection, entry control points, checkpoints, convoys, and maritime ports and security zones.

**Capability Effect:** Optical impairment.

## (U) LROI cont.

(U) **Delivery Systems:** TBD

(FOUO) **Collateral Damage:** Potential for eye damage if exposed within NOHD.

(FOUO) **Counter Measures:** Filtering goggles.

(FOUO) **Environmental Effects:** Reduced effect during daylight, fog, and rain. During daylight-moderate glare, no flash blindness, some afterimage.

(U) **Policy Implications:** See NLW Policy References (Optical Distractors).

(U) **Unique Logistics:** None

## Distributed Sound and Light Array (DSLA)

**Status:** Prototype
**Lead Agency:** JNLWD

**Target Type:** Counter-Personnel

**Intended Target Response:** Deny access into/out of an area to individuals, move individuals through an area, and suppress individuals.

**Description:** DSLA uses a combined laser, non-coherent light, and acoustics to produce a synergistic engagement system.

**Concept of Employment:** Hail, warn, and/or deter individuals and vehicle operators from approaching entry control points, mobile patrols/convoys, and vehicle checkpoints.

**Capability Effect:** Optical and auditory impairment and/or intelligible audible tones.

## *(U) DSLA cont.*

(U) **Delivery Systems:** Vehicle, trailer, or ground mounted.

(FOUO) **Collateral Damage:** Potential for eye damage if exposed within Nominal Ocular Hazard Distance and potential for auditory damage if over exposed at close range.

(FOUO) **Counter Measures:** Filtering goggles and hearing protection (earplugs) may reduce or negate effects.

(FOUO) **Environmental Effects:** Reduced effect during wind, fog, and rain. During daylight-moderate glare, no flash blindness, some afterimage.

(U) **Policy Implications:** See NLW Policy References (Optical Distractors).

(U) **Unique Logistics:** None

## *Nano-second Electrical Pulses*

Status: Conceptual
Lead Agency: JNLWD

Target Type: Counter-Personnel

Intended Target Response: Disable individuals.

**Description:** An electrical waveform, with the potential to substantially increase the duration of disabling effects compared to existing HEMI capabilities.

**Concept of Employment:** Force protection, crowd control, detainee operations, patrols/convoys, building clearing, and other offensive and defensive operations.

**Capability Effect:** Electro-muscular incapacitation (i.e., the loss of voluntary muscular control by electrical stimulation).

# X26 TASER®

| | Currently fielded by USMC, USN, USAF and USA: COTS item, result of Operational Needs Statement (ONS). Lead Agency: USA |
|---|---|
| | Target Type: Counter-Personnel |
| | Intended Target Response: Disable an individual. |

**Description:** An electro-muscular incapacitation (EMI) device that uses a nitrogen air cartridge propulsion system to launch two probes tethered to an electrically charged cartridge. Effective range is 0-35 ft. depending on cartridge type, penetrates up to 2 inches of clothing.

**Concept of Employment:** Force protection and other operations that require the ability to totally disable an individual.

**Capability Effect:** Human electro-muscular incapacitation (i.e., the loss of voluntary muscular control by electrical stimulation).

# (U) X26 TASER® cont.

 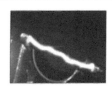 

(U)

(U) **Delivery System:** Handheld or weapon mounted.

(FOUO) **Collateral Damage:** Potential for injuries when individual falls, minor surface burns at probe sites, and possible ignition of flammable liquids or gas if hit by probes.

(FOUO) **Counter Measures:** Plywood or hard/shatter resistant shields.

(FOUO) **Environmental Effects:** Potential EMI to operator if discharged during heavy rain.

(U) **Policy Implications:** See NLW Policy References (Human Electro-Muscular Incapacitation Devices)

(U) **Unique Logistics:** Cartridge replacements; equipment maintenance; battery pack recharging/replacement.

## *Subsurface Non-Lethal Engagement - Impulse Swimmer Gun*

**Anticipated Fielding**: TBD
**Status**: Developmental
**Lead Agency**: USN

**Target Type**: Counter-Personnel

**Intended Target Response**: Deny access into/out of an area and suppress underwater swimmers and divers.

**Description**: A tethered transducer cable connected to a control unit and an air gun and spark gap generator that emits a directional, underwater pulsed sound wave. Weight is 50 lbs and effective range is between 0-150 m.

**Concept of Employment**: Force protection, port security to prevent unauthorized underwater activities.

**Capability Effect**: Auditory impairment and/or nausea.

## *(U) Subsurface Non-Lethal Engagement - Impulse Swimmer Gun cont.*

(U)    No minimum safe engagement range                    Maximum Effective Range  150 meters

(U) **Delivery System**: Deployed from pier side.

(FOUO) **Collateral Damage**: Potential for auditory damage if over exposed at close range and impact on aquatic life.

(FOUO) **Counter Measures**: Neoprene wetsuit may slightly attenuate noise/effect.

(FOUO) **Environmental Effects**: Background noise (harbor/boat engine noise) can reduce effects.

(U) **Policy Implications**: None

(U) **Unique Logistics**: None

## Enhanced Underwater Loudhailer (eLOUD©)

| |
|---|
| **Currently fielded by USCG and USN:** COTS item.<br>**Lead Agency:** USCG |
| **Target Type:** Counter-Personnel |
| **Intended Target Response:** Deny access into/out of an area and suppress underwater swimmers and divers. |
| **Description:** Man portable, easy to operate unit comprised of a control unit and a 75 ft transducer cable with 8 inch transducers spaced 24 inches apart. Unit transmits intelligible commands up to 2 hours with a battery source, to a distance of 457 m and depth of 40 m. |

**Concept of Employment:** Deployable from pier or vessel for force protection and port operations/security to prevent unauthorized underwater activities.

**Capability Effect:** Auditory impairment and/or intelligible audible tones.

## (U) eLOUD© cont.

(U)                                                             Maximum Effective Range: 457 meters

(U) **Delivery System:** Vessel and pier side delivery.

(FOUO) **Collateral Damage:** Potential for auditory damage if over exposed and potential impact on aquatic life.

(FOUO) **Counter Measures:** Neoprene wetsuit may slightly attenuate noise/effect. Hearing protection (earplugs) may reduce or negate effects.

(FOUO) **Environmental Effects:** Background noise can reduce effects (harbor/vessel engine sounds).

(U) **Policy Implications:** None

(U) **Unique Logistics:** None

## *Multi-Frequency RF Vehicle Stopper*

| | |
|---|---|
| **Anticipated Fielding:** FY18<br>**Status:** Development<br>**Lead Agency:** JNLWD | |
| **Target Type:** Counter-Materiel | |
| **Intended Target Response:** Stop vehicles. | |

**Description:** A portable RF Vehicle Stopper system would allow for the maintenance of a safe, non-lethal keep-out zone by using high power microwaves to disrupt vehicle engines.

**Concept of Employment:** Force protection, access control points, roadblocks, and checkpoints to stop vehicles.

**Capabilities Effect:** Disrupts vehicle electrical components to cause the engine to stall.

## *(U) Multi-Frequency RF Vehicle Stopper cont.*

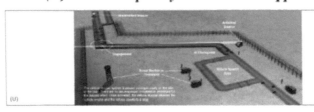

(U) **Delivery System:** Self-contained, mobile/transportable system.

(FOUO) **Collateral Damage:** Collateral effects against unintended targets in the immediate target area.

(FOUO) **Counter Measures:** Shielding or hardening of equipment.

(FOUO) **Environmental Effects:** None

(U) **Policy Implications:** None

(U) **Unique Logistics:** None

## *Pre-emplaced Electric Vehicle Stopper (PEVS)*

| | |
|---|---|
| **Status:** Prototype | |
| **Lead Agency:** JNLWD | |
| **Target Type:** Counter-Materiel | |
| **Intended Target Response:** Stop and disable vehicles. | |

**Description:** A pre-emplaced, non-intrusive device that provides an electrical pulse through deployed contacts to shutdown power train electrical circuits or components.

**Concept of Employment:** Force protection at vehicle checkpoints to stop vehicles and most effective when used in concert with barrier or entanglement system to slow vehicle momentum.

**Capability Effect:** Disrupts vehicle electrical components to cause the engine to stall.

# ACOUSTIC TRAUMA: BIO EFFECTS OF SOUND:

"Noise is violence: it disturbs. To make noise is to interrupt a transmission, to disconnect, to kill."

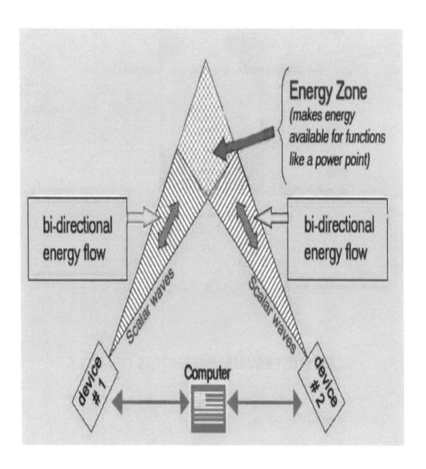

# REFERENCES

**Microwave Mind Control Symptoms & Published Evidence**

[**Editor's Note:** The following report from Cheryl Welsh provides a listing of some of the reported symptoms of electronic microwave mind control technologies, published evidence of their existence, and demonstrated military interest and/or funding for these technologies. Many of these electronic mind control developments were perfected at Montauk, Long Island in the 1960's, 70's, and 80's in a privately funded operation known as The Montauk Project. Al Bielek, Preston Nichols, Peter Moon, Stewart Swerdlow, and others have written and reported extensively on the details of this project. These energies can be beamed to large populations from aircraft, helicopters, satellites, and land-based microwave towers, which have proliferated worldwide at an explosive rate in the past two years. For more background info on mind control, read our introductory page Mind Control, The Ultimate Terror (http://educate-yourself.org/mc/) ...Ken Adachi]

**Source:** Cheryl Welsh <welsh@dcn.davis.ca.us>

http://educate-yourself.org/mc/listofmcsymptoms05jun03.shtml

**March, 2003**

## Reported Symptoms

1.  Microwave hearing

2.  Transmission of specific commands into the subconscious

3.  Visual disturbances, visual hallucinations

4.  Inject words, numbers into brain via electromagnetic radiation waves

5.  Manipulation of emotions

6.  Reading thoughts remotely

7.  Causing pain to any nerve of the body.

8.  Remote manipulation of human behavior from space

9.  Harassment, stress symptoms such as helicopters flying overhead

10. Seeing, as in a camera, through your eyes, i.e. to see what you see exactly

11. Control of sleep patterns.

12. Computer-brain interface, control and communication

13. Complex control of the brain such as retrieving memories, implanting personalities

## Symptoms, Published Evidence, and Military Interest/Funding

### Symptom

1. Microwave hearing. The hearing of voices in the head from an outside source, but nobody else can hear the voices except the targeted individual.

### Published Evidence

A. Ultrascience III, Spies are us. Featured Dr. James C. Lin, Ph.D. biomedical and electrical engineer, educator, author of Microwave Auditory Effects and Applications, 1978. Lin demonstrated microwave hearing, a symptom of many of the victims, hearing voices. Also featured Cheryl Welsh on the issue of mind control experimentation.

B. International Defense Review, 3-1-1993, Special Operations Survives Pentagon Budget Constraints, by Ramon Lopez.

"JASORS, Joint Advanced Special Operations Radio System is being developed by Harris Corporation. ...is a very ambitious, leading-edge technology program, ...Whiles JASORS is a near-term SOF, [Special Operations Forces] enhancement, SORDAC, [Special Operations Research Development and Acquisition Center], is also investigating long-range (1998-2010) and "far-future" (2011 and beyond) weaponry and support equipment. [SORDAC's director, Army Colonel Douglas J.] Richardson said one far-future communications system being investigated is "synthetic telepathy." One day, SOF commandos may be capable of communicating through thought processes."

C. Margo Cherney FOIA request for complete NASA abstract Report Number: AD-A090426, June 1, 1980. Response from Brooks Air Force Base, Jan.25, 2000: The requested information is fully denied under 5 U.S.C. 552(b)(1). NASA abstract in part stated,

"A decoy and deception concept presently being considered is to remotely create the perception of noise in the heads of personnel by exposing them to low power, pulsed microwave. When people are illuminated with properly modulated low power microwaves the sensation is reported as a buzzing, clicking, or hissing which seems to originate (regardless of the person's position in the field) within or just behind the head. The phenomena occur at average power densities as low as microwatts per square centimeter with carrier frequencies from 0.4 to 3.0 GHz. [within frequency range of 400 Mega Hertz (MHz) to 3 Giga Hertz] By proper choice of pulse characteristics, intelligible speech may be created. Before this technique may be extended and used for military applications, an understanding of the basic principles must be developed. Such an understanding is not only required to optimize the use of the concept for camouflage, decoy and deception operations but is required to properly assess safety factors of such microwave exposure."

D.  Microwave News, editor, Louis Slesin, Jan/Feb 1997 p 14. U.S. Air Force Looks to the Battlefields of the Future: Electromagnetic Fields That Might "Boggle the Mind"

"It would also appear possible to create high fidelity speech in the human body, raising the possibility of covert suggestion and psychological direction. When a high-power microwave pulse in the GHz range strikes the human body, a very small temperature perturbation occurs. This is associated with a sudden expansion of the slightly heated tissue. This expansion is fast enough to produce an acoustic wave. If a pulse stream is used, it should be possible to create an internal acoustic field in the 5-15 kHz range, which is audible. Thus, it may be possible to "talk" to selected adversaries in a fashion that would be most disturbing to them."

E.  Federal Times, Dec. 13, 1976 Microwave Weapons Study by Soviets Cited: The Defense Intelligence Agency has released a report on heavy Communist research on microwaves, including their use as weapons. Microwaves are used in radar, television and microwave ovens. They can cause disorientation and possibly heart attacks in humans. Another biological effect with possible anti-personnel uses is ' microwave hearing.'

"Sounds and possibly even words which appear to be originating intra-cranially (within the head) can be induced by signal modulation at very low average power densities," the report said. According to the study, Communist work in this area "has great potential for development into a system for disorienting or disrupting the behavior patterns of military or diplomatic personnel."

No mention was made of the still-unexplained microwave bombardment of the American Embassy in Moscow. The study dealt largely with long-term exposure of days or weeks in industrial situations, which usually produce mild effects. Short exposure to intense radiation can cause heart seizure and a wide range of physical disorders.

**Military interest or funding**

A. Yes. See above.


## Symptom

2. Transmission of specific commands into the subconscious

   **Published Evidence**

   A. Defense News, US Explores Russian Mind Control Technology by Barbara Opall, January, 11-17-1993, p. 4.

   "Pioneered by the government-funded Department of Psycho-Correction at the Moscow Medical Academy, acoustic psycho-correction involves the transmission of specific commands via static or white noise bands into the human subconscious without upsetting other intellectual functions.

Experts said laboratory demonstrations have shown encouraging results after exposure of less than one minute."

B. Janet Morris, reported in the book, The Sorcerer's Challenge: Fears and Hopes for the Weapons of the Next Millennium, by David Shukman. London: Hodder & Stoughton, page 223. of demonstration shown on BBC television on news program entitled Newsnight by David Shukman, (tape available on request).

C. U.S. News, January 3-10, 2000, John Norseen [Lockheed Martin neuro-engineer in Intelligent Systems Division], Reading your Mind and Injecting Smart Thoughts by Douglas Pasternak.

"Norseen's interest in the brain stems from a Soviet book he read in the mid-1980s, claiming that research on the mind would revolutionize the military and society at large. [He] coined the term "Bio-fusion" to cover his plans to map and manipulate [the brain] leading to advances in ...national security... and ...would be able to convert thoughts into computer commands by deciphering the brain's electrical activity. Bio-Fusion would reveal the fingerprints of the brain by using mathematical models, [Smirnov's computer program uses mathematical models also]. It sounds crazy, The National Aeronautics and Space Administration, the Defense Advanced Research Projects Agency, ...have all awarded...research contracts to Norseen. Norseen is waiting to hear if the second stage of these contracts-portions of them classified- comes through. Norseen's theories are grounded in current science. ...By MRI [Magnetic Resonant Imaging], scientists can tell what the person was doing at the time of the recording...Emotions from love to hate can be recognized from the brain's electrical activity. ...Norseen predicts profiling by brain print will be in place by 2005.

...Norseen would like to draw upon Russian brain-mimicking software and American brain -mapping breakthroughs to allow that communication to take place in a less invasive way. A modified helmet could record a pilot's brainwaves. 'When you say right 090 degrees...the computer would see that electrical pattern in the brain and turn the plane 090 degrees. If the pilot misheard instructions to turn 090 degrees and was thinking "080 degrees," the helmet would detect the error, then inject the right number via electromagnetic waves.'"

**Military interest or funding**

A. Yes, Defense Electronics, DOD, Intel Agencies Look at Russian Mind Control... by Mark Tapscott, July, 1993 p. 17.

"In a series of closed meetings...FBI officials were briefed on the decade-long research on a computerized acoustic device allegedly capable of implanting thoughts in a person's mind without that person being aware of the thought."

Also, US corp. buys Russian mind control equipment.

## Symptom

3. Visual disturbances, visual hallucinations.

**Published Evidence**

A. CNN TV: A demonstration by Dr. Elizabeth Rauscher and Dr. William van Bise, directed magnetic signals into the brain of reporter Chuck DeCaro. They created visual images as in a hallucination. This program also features Dr. Robert O. Becker, two time Nobel prize nominee, scientist and researcher of electromagnetic radiation effects on the body and author of Body Electric, summarized, "The government has never disproved the psychological effects of electromagnetic radiation. "Dr. Robert Becker commented "that this is a substantial step forward in the understanding how the visual system works" and would be a powerful weapon if used on fighter pilots while trying to fly."

For a 55$ copy of this tape call CNN at 404-827-2712 and ask for R2501 #13, R2747 #33, R2501 #15, R2501-#17. It runs about 20 minutes.

**Military interest or funding**

A. Yes. See above.

## Symptom

4. Inject words, numbers into brain via EMR waves

   **Published Evidence**

   A. Defense News, US Explores Russian Mind Control Technology by Barbara Opall January, 11-17-1993, p. 4.

      "Experts said laboratory demonstrations have shown encouraging results after exposure of less than one minute."

   B. U.S. News, 1-3-2000, John Norseen, Reading and changing your mind...ibid see Symptom 2, section C.

   C. Lobster Magazine, Mind Control and the American Government by Martin Cannon, Number 23. J.F. Schapitz was conducting classified work on microwaving the subconscious with commands as in hypnosis. This work is classified.

   **Military interest or funding**

   A. Defense News, US Explores Russian Mind Control Technology by Barbara Opall, January, 11-17-1993, p. 4.

      "Moreover, decades of research and investment of untold millions of rubles in the process of psycho-correction has produced the ability to alter behavior on willing and unwilling subjects, the experts add. ...Russian senior research scientist, diplomats, ...are beginning to provide limited demonstrations for their U.S. counterparts. Further evaluations of key technologies in the United States are being planned, as are discussions aimed at creating a frame-work for bringing the issue under bilateral or multilateral controls, U.S. and Russian sources say."

## Symptom

5. Manipulation of emotions

   **Published Evidence**

   A. Ultra science, Weapons of War, The Learning Channel, 1997, Featured Dr. Michael Persinger, Laurentian University, Canada. Dr. Persinger described weapons using "psycho or influence technology" and electromagnetic radiation frequencies to control what people think, for psychological warfare purposes.

   B. Ultrascience, War 2020, Beyond Productions, The Learning Channel, 1998, with Dr. Michael Persinger, Laurentian University performed a demonstration of a helmet with solenoids which induce magnetic fields into the brain and cause panic, fear, God and UFO experiences. He stated that with current technology it is possible to use mind control on the mass populations.

   **Military interest or funding**

   A. Yes. See above.

## Symptom

6. Reading thoughts remotely

   **Published Evidence**

A. Nature Vol 391/22 January 1998 Advances in Neuroscience May Threaten Human Rights by Declan Butler.

"...at the annual public meeting of the French national bioethics committee held last week in Paris... Jean-Pierre Changeux, the chairman of the committee and a neuroscientist at the Institute Pasteur in Paris, told the meeting that understanding the working of the human brain is likely to become one of the most ambitious and rich disciplines of the future. But neuroscience also poses potential risks, he said, arguing that advances in cerebral imaging make the scope for invasion of privacy immense. Although the equipment needed is still highly specialized, it will become commonplace and capable of being used at a distance, he predicted. That will open the way for abuses such as invasion of personal liberty, control of behavior and brainwashing. These are far from being science-fiction concerns, said Changeux, and constitute "a serious risk to society". "Denis LeBihan, a researcher at the French Atomic Energy Commission, told the meeting that the use of imaging techniques has reached the stage where "we can almost read people's thoughts".

B. Signal Magazine, October, 2001, article titled Decoding Minds by Dr. John D. Norseen, of Lockheed Martin stated,

"We are at the point where this database has been developed enough that we can use a single electrode or something like an airport security system where there is a dome above our head to get enough information that we can know the number you're thinking,"

C. US News and World Report Jan 3-10, 2000, "Reading your Mind and Injecting Smart Thoughts" by Douglas Pasternak, p. 67 quotes John Norseen,

"...Norseen's theories are grounded in current science."

D. The Washington Times, August 17, 2002, the article entitled NASA Plans to Read Terrorist's Minds at Airport stated,

"Airport security screeners may soon try to read the minds of travelers to identify terrorists. Officials of the National Aeronautics and Space Administration [NASA] have told Northwest Airlines security specialists that the agency is developing brain-monitoring devices in cooperation with a commercial firm, which it did not identify. Space technology would be adapted to receive and analyze brain-wave and heartbeat patterns, then feed that data into computerized programs 'to detect passengers who potentially might pose a threat,' according to briefing documents obtained by The Washington Times. NASA wants to use 'noninvasive neuro-electric sensors,' imbedded in gates, to collect tiny electric signals that all brains and hearts transmit. Computers would apply statistical algorithms to correlate physiologic patterns with computerized data on travel routines, criminal background and credit information from 'hundreds to thousands of data sources,' NASA documents say. ...Robert Park, spokesman for the American Physical Society stated, 'We're close to the point where they can tell to an extent what you're thinking about by which part of the brain is activated, which is close to reading your mind. ...The idea is plausible, he says, but frightening'.

E. Science Digest 7-84 page 30 quoting Thomas Jensen of Chicago's Rush-Presbyterian St. Luke's Medical Center, and Donald York

"we have discovered that just before a person says a particular word, the brain emits waves peculiar to that word alone. ...These waves are the same from person to person."

F. Think, Sept/Oct 1992 Dr. Richard Clark at the Flinders University of South Australia wrote the following:

"Artificial neural network computer programs are used to include the ability to learn and recognize simple patterns of thought from the electrical fields of the brain."

G.  Science Digest Oct. 1981 entitled Machines that read Minds by Gary Selden stated that

"Indeed, CIA spokespeople have admitted 'following' ERP [This is the waveform that the brain characteristically emits after absorbing an external event] research, perhaps the way the agency followed LSD research in the 1950s. ...With remote monitors, such an instrument would be a spy's dream." It is naive to think that the CIA has not exploited this research.

H.  Nature, 1-22-1998 The national bioethics committee is taking such threats so seriously that it is launching a study. The title of this article was Advances in Neuroscience May Threaten Human Rights. Denis Le Bihan, a researcher at the French Atomic Energy Commission, stated

"we can almost read people's thoughts".

I.  New Scientist, 12-11-1999 Vol. 164, No. 2216 page 25 by Graham-Rowe, Duncan, described the technology as a computer programmed under the notion that most people behave in predictable ways when walking to their car. This behavior is transferred into a mathematical pattern and the computer recognizes it as such.

"Anyone who deviates from this set pattern, such as someone who walks in circles or who lurks in shadows, will set off an alarm..."

This is just a small example of human behavior and how it is studied scientifically. No doubt with the political will and the money of national security defense, as victims are alleging, human behavior has been studied and is controlled by government technology.

**Military interest or funding**

A. Yes, government funded. U.S News and World Report, Jan 3-10, 2000, John Norseen, Reading Your Mind and Injecting Smart Thoughts by Douglas Pasternak, p. 67

"...It sounds crazy, but Uncles Sam is listening. the National Aeronautics and Space Administration, The Defense Advanced Research Projects Agency, and the Army's National Ground Intelligence Center have all awarded small basic research contracts to Norseen, who works for Lockheed-Martin's Intelligent Systems Division. Norseen is waiting to hear if the second stage of these contracts -portions of them classified-come through. "

## Symptom

7. Causing pain to any nerve of the body

**Published Evidence**

A. Bulletin of Atomic Scientist, Sept 1994, Softkill Fallacy by Steve Aftergood, Page 45. Barbara Hatch Rosenberg writes:

"Many of the non-lethal weapons under consideration utilize infrasound or electromagnetic energy (including lasers, microwave or radio-frequency radiation, or visible light pulsed at brain-wave frequency) for their effects. These weapons are said to cause temporary or permanent blinding, interference with mental processes, modification of behavior and emotional response, seizures, severe pain, dizziness, nausea and diarrhea, or disruption of internal organ functions in various other ways."

B. Marine Corps Times, March 5, 2001, p. 10., The People Zapper by C. Mark Brinkley,

"...focuses energy into a beam of micro-millimeter waves designed to stop an individual in his tracks. ...The energy, which falls near microwaves on the electromagnetic spectrum, causes moisture in a person's skin to heat up rapidly, creating a burning sensation..."

C. Numerous other articles on nonlethal weapons, see CAHRA website: www.dcn.davis.ca.us/~welsh

**Military Interest or funding**

A. Yes, government funding and very heavily discussed.

## Symptom

8. Remote manipulation of human behavior from space

**Published Evidence**

A. Journal of Microwave Power, 12(4) 1977, p. 320. Radiation Bio-effects Research by Dodge and Glaser,

"The information explosion in this field has been quite dramatic since 1969, when the international data base was estimated to consist of less than 1,000 citations. In addition to maintaining inventories of the literature, we have undertaken from time to time to provide assessments of international trends in research, development, and occupational health and safety. In the present paper, we will concentrate on events which have transpired since our last review effort in 1975. Major events which have taken place during that period include: ... (5) Unpublished analyses of microwave bio-effects literature which were disseminated to Congress and to other officials arguing the case for remote control of human behavior by radar;

B. Moscow Rabochaya Tribuna, Nov. 26, 1994, FBIS, Ref # MM3011130594 Psychotronic Arms Potential Must be Monitored, by Anatoliy Pushenko, member of the Russian Federation of Space Exploration Scientific and Technical Council:

"A prominent specialist speaks for the first time in our press in Rabochaya Tribuna about psychotropic weapons, which started to be developed in the sixties--space-based energy systems capable of killing every living thing on the planet and driving millions of people crazy. ... There are frequencies that are beneficial to people, but naturally there are also those which are hazardous. ...That is, it has a direct physical effect on the human brain. ... The terrible danger of psychotropic weapons is the possibility of their simultaneously and unequivocally affecting large masses of people over huge areas.

C. Moscow Armeyskiy Sbornik, Oct. 1996, No. 10. P. 88-98, FBIS, Russian article, Mori DocID: 587170, Russia: National Information Security by Russian Major General, Valeriy Menshikov, doctor of technical sciences, and Colonel Boris Rodionov.,

"...Thus, the new space systems are potentially dangerous from the aspect of unfolding a wide-scale 'information war' and even creating global systems for controlling people's behavior in any region, ..."

D. FBIS [Foreign Broadcast Information Service] article by Alain Gossens: Apocalypse Now? HAARP... report from Brussels Telemoustique, 1997, FBIS MoriDocID 587140, scientists, weapons experts, EU members on U.S HAARP Project

"Are the Americans currently developing a vast weapons system capable of scanning the entrails of the earth to seek out secret bases, jamming any form of radio communications, influencing human behavior... Nevertheless, if one is aware of the fact that the real sponsors are the Navy, the Air Force, and the Department of Defense, then it is hard to believe that it is not a project for military purposes."

**Military interest or funding**

A.  Probably. See tracking of airplanes, tracking by GPS. Satellites capable of taking pictures of license plates, etc.

## Symptom

9.  Harassment, stress symptoms such as helicopters flying overhead

**Published Evidence**

A.  The Sorcerer's Challenge: Fears and Hopes for the Weapons of the Next Millennium, Shukman, David, London: Hodder & Stoughton, 1995, P. 225 [Ref. Waco siege in 1993]

> "The best they [FBI] they could do was to maintain a barrage of noise with helicopters and loudspeakers to keep the followers awake and to try to undermine their [Koresh and follower's} morale."

B.  Aviation Week & Space Technology 1-19-1998 p.55 on information warfare and US capabilities.

> "...techniques as esoteric as 'mapping the psychological and cognitive makeup' of foreign leaders or key groups in order to predict reactions to manipulated information, ...".

C.  Aviation Week & Space Technology 3-9-1998, page 21 stated that [ref. USAF Gen. John Jumper]

> "Jumper talked about tools that could...make potential enemies see, hear and believe things that don't exist"

> The military is discussing the deployment of weapons to do just that, create symptoms of mental illness. And yet this information is not taken seriously by professionals and has not been accepted as relevant to victim's allegations.

D. Excerpts from CAHRA website:
www.dcn.davis.ca.us/~welsh. Quotes from military journals
and government document:

1. 1."...to control the will and perception of adversaries ...by
applying a regime of shock and awe...It is about effecting
behavior."

2. "A decoy and deception concept [using microwaves] to
"create intelligible speech 'in the head, 'raising the
possibility of covert suggestion and psychological
direction."

3. "tools that could...make potential enemies see, hear and
believe things that don't exist."

4. "...crowd control and urban warfare devices that
temporarily could paralyze an entire village."

**Military interest and funding**

A. Yes. See above.

<u>Symptom</u>

10. Seeing, as in a camera, through your eyes, i.e. to see what you see
exactly

**Published Evidence**

A. BBC News Online Oct 11, 1999, Looking Through Cats' Eyes
Fuzzy, But Recognizable, Dr. David Whitehouse, A BBC
News article reported on the first pictures from an experiment
to see through the eyes of a cat.

http://news.bbc.co.uk/hi/english/sci/tech/newsid
471000/471786.stm

**Military interest and feasibility**

10. Unknown.

## Symptom

11. Control of sleep patterns

**Published Evidence**

A. CNN news broadcast, Special Assignment, Nov.-1985, by Chuck DeCaro, Weapons of War, Is there an RF Gap? Dr. Ross Adey discussed a demonstration of the 1950s Russian Lida machine, which used electromagnetic energy to put Russian psychiatric patients to sleep, as a substitute for tranquilizers and to treat neurotic disturbances. Dr. Adey stated that it worked on cats and dogs and put them to sleep.

B. The Defense and Foreign Affairs Daily, Jun 7, 1983, Vol. XII, Number 104, Psy War: Soviet Device Experiment by Dr. Stefan T. Possony reported: "...Dr. Ross Adey, chief of research at Loma Linda...started testing the machine [the Lida] ...the device is on loan to Dr. Ross Adey. 'The machine is technically described as 'a distant pulse treatment apparatus. It generates 40 megahertz radio waves which stimulate the brain's electromagnetic activity at substantially lower frequencies"

**Military interest or funding**

A. Yes. The Defense and Foreign Affairs Daily, Jun 7, 1983, Vol. XII, Number 104, Psy-War: Soviet Device Experiment by Dr. Stefan T. Possony.

"...On April 29, 1983 this author, as a participant in a panel at the Defense '83 conference sponsored by Defense and Foreign Affairs, reported on Dr. Adey's work...These remarks were delivered to a panel studying psychological warfare."

## Symptom

12. Computer-brain interface, control and communication

### Published Evidence

A. APPROPRIATION/BUDGET ACTIVITY RDT&E, Defense-wide BA2 Applied Research R-1 ITEM NOMENCLATURE Computing Systems and Communications Technology PE 0602301E, Project ST-19 The Augmented Cognition (AugCog) program will develop the means to measure a subject's cognitive state in real time and manipulate it to accomplish the functions. The goal of the Augmented Cognition program is to develop methods that integrate digital devices that support memory, perception, and thinking, and link that support with the user's context state information to directly improve the overall cognitive performance of the warfighter. The Perceptual Processing Display program focuses on exploiting neuroscience and perceptual processing technologies to redesign devices that deliver information to the human perceptual system. These new devices will be able to extract relevant signal from extraneous background noise, through perceptual modeling. This program will develop technologies that simplify relevant, and eliminate irrelevant, information to improve perception, comprehension, memory, inference, and decision-making. Specifically, this program will demonstrate the manipulation of perceptual data along hundreds of dimensions of the human perceptual system, and will result in the doubling of human information processing performance.

http://www.darpa.mil/body/pdf/FY03BudEst.pdf

### Military interest

12. Yes. See above.

## Symptom

13. Complex control of the brain such as retrieving memories, implanting personalities

### Published Evidence

A. Converging Technologies for Improving Human Performance, A National Science Foundation /U.S. Department of Commerce-sponsored report (2002). Relevant excerpts. Full text at http://itri.loyola.edu/ConvergingTechnologies/Report/NBIC_pre_publication.pdf

List of Participants and Contributors included NASA, Office of Naval Research, DARPA, Sandia National Labs, USAF Research Labs, Raytheon, Lucent Technologies, MIT and Stanford.

i. Expanding Human Cognition and Communication. Page 85.

"...Truly, the mind is the final frontier, and unraveling its mysteries will have tremendous practical benefits. ...Failure to invest in the necessary multidisciplinary research would delay or even prevent these benefits to the economy, to national security, and to individual well-being. Rapid recent progress in cognitive science and related fields has brought us to the point where we could achieve several breakthroughs that would be of great value to mankind. ...For example, progress in the cognitive neuroscience of the human brain has been achieved through new research methodologies, based in both biology and information science, such as functional magnetic resonance imagining (fMRI) and infrared sensors. However, we are reaching the resolution limits of current instrumentation, for example because of concerns about the safety of human research subjects (Food and Drug Administration 1998), so progress will stall quickly unless breakthroughs in NBIC can give us research tools with much greater resolution, sensitivity, and capacity to analyze data."

ii.     Page 86. The Human Cognome Project.

"It is time to launch a Human Cognome Project, comparable to the successful Human Genome Project, to chart the structure and functions of the human mind. No project would be more fundamental to progress throughout science and engineering, or would require a more complete unification of NBIC sciences. ...While the research would include a complete mapping of the connections in the human brain, it would be far more extensive than neuroscience. ...Some participants in the human cognition and communication working group were impressed by the long-term potential for uploading aspects of individual personality to computers and robots, thereby expanding the scope of human experience, action, and longevity."

iii.    Page 88. Statements and Visions

"Participants in the human cognition and communication panel contributed a number of statements, describing the current situation and suggesting strategies for building upon it, as well as transformative visions of what could be accomplished in ten or twenty years through a concentrated effort."

iv.     Page 287 National Security, Theme Summary.

"...Investment in convergent Nanotechnology, Biotechnology, Information technology and Cognitive science [NBIC] is expected to result in innovative technologies that revolutionize many domains of conflict and peacekeeping. ...As former Defense Secretary William J. Perry has noted, these are the technological breakthroughs that are 'Changing the face of war and how we prepare for war.' There are numerous special programs, reports and presentations that address these goals. The Department of Defense has designated nanoscience as a strategic research area in order to accelerate the expected benefits (Murday 1999). ...Applications of brain-machine interface. The convergence of all four NBIC fields will give warfighters the ability to control complex entities by sending control actions prior to thoughts (cognition) being fully formed. The intent is to take brain signals (nanotechnology for augmented sensitivity and nonintrusive signal detection) and use them in a control strategy (information technology), and then impart back into the brain the sensations of feedback signals (biotechnology)."

B.  In Approaching the 21st Century: Opportunities for NIMH Neuroscience Research, The National Advisory Mental Health Council Report to Congress on the Decade of the Brain, Jan. 1988 by USHHS. Page 49 stated

"Several investigators had noted that when neurons were given brief but intense high-frequency stimulation their electrical properties were changed in ways that would fit those proposed for memory: The changes were triggered by an electrical event, they were strengthened by repetition, and they persisted indefinitely. ...the scientists found that intense high-frequency pulses trigger an unusually large release of calcium in the post synaptic cell..."

**Military interest or funding**

14. Yes. See above.

(Thank you to those who sent me much of this information: Tessa Puglia, Harlan Girard, Margo Cherney, and John Ginter.)

Cheryl Welsh, March, 2003

For more information, visit Citizens Against Human Rights Abuse (CAHRA): www.dcn.davis.ca.us/~welsh

# Other books by this author in the Mind Control Technology Book Series:

- ➢ Book One - "Remote Brain Targeting"

- ➢ Book Two - "You Are Not My Big Brother"

- ➢ Book Three – "Covert Technological Murder -Targeted"

- ➢ Book Four – "Diary of an Angry Targeted Individual"

- ➢ Book Five – "The Targeting of Myron May – Florida State University Gunman"

- ➢ Book Six – Deceived Beyond Belief: Prologue

- ➢ Also, by same author, the inspirational metaphysical book:

- ➢ Book Seven - "The Heart is Another Name for God – Lotus Dream"


## AUTHOR'S WEBSITE

http://www.bigbrotherwatchingus.com

Interior images courtesy of Freedigitalphotos.net


HANG IN THERE!

Made in United States
Troutdale, OR
11/29/2023

15120441R00146